GOD HAS A PLAN FOR

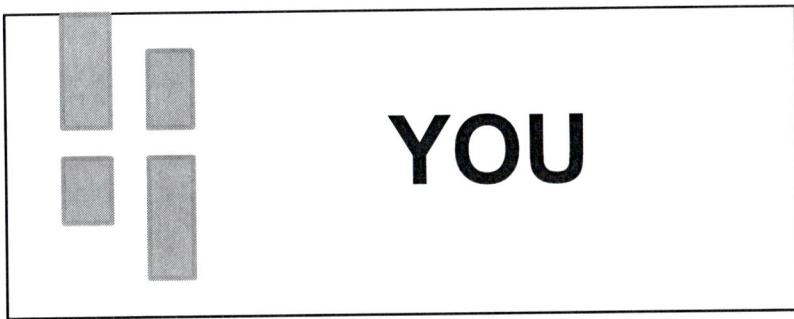

SELF-GOVERNMENT

For I know the plans I have for you," declares the LORD, "plans to prosper you and not to harm you, plans to give you hope and a future.
Jeremiah 29:11

By David Lange

GOD HAS A PLAN FOR YOU
SELF-GOVERNMENT
By David E. Lange

Copyright © 2014 David E. Lange

All rights reserved. No portion of this book may be reproduced, stored in a retrieval system, or transmitted in any form or by any means—electronic, mechanical, photocopy, recording, scanning, or other—except for brief quotations in critical reviews or articles, without the prior written permission of the publisher.

Unless otherwise indicated, Scripture quotations are taken from the HOLY BIBLE: NEW INTERNATIONAL VERSION®. © 1973, 1978, 1984 International Bible Society. Used by permission of Zondervan. All rights reserved.

Scripture quotations marked NLT are taken from the *Holy Bible*, New Living Translation, copyright 1996, 2004. Used by permission of Tyndale House Publishers, Inc., Wheaton, Illinois 60189. All rights reserved.

Published by Lange Publishing, Pacific, MO
Library of Congress Control Number: 2014911672
ISBN 978-0-9824070-2-8
ISBN 0-9824070-2-5
Printed in the United States of America

This book is dedicated to . . .

Christy. She is my wonderful, supportive, and beautiful wife. Without the support of her and my awesome kids, Jeremiah, Bethany, Sofia, Bentley, and Blake this work would not have been possible.

Dad and Mom. I cherish the godly parents that I have been blessed with.

Mission Community Church. I also want to acknowledge and thank our church family for putting up with me during this process.

Debra. My very supportive sister, her family, Jon Marc, Nathan, Micah, and Natalie.

Of course the greatest honor and glory goes to Jesus Christ, my Lord and Savior!

For more information check out
WWW.BIBLEISTHEROCK.COM

If you were blessed by this series check out
WWW.FIVECOMMITMENTS.COM

CONTENTS

MUST READ INTRODUCTION ... 1

TEN SELF-GOVERNMENT LIFE TRUTHS ... 9

SELF-GOVERNMENT 1
SCRIPTURE ALONE IS WHAT GOVERNS US ... 13

SELF-GOVERNMENT 2
WE NEED A NEW NATURE ... 27

SELF-GOVERNMENT 3
WE MUST CRUCIFY OUR OLD NATURE ... 45

SELF-GOVERNMENT 4
I AM CREATED TO SERVE ... 63

SELF-GOVERNMENT 5
I AM CREATED TO PRAISE ... 83

SELF-GOVERNMENT 6
I AM CREATED TO ENCOURAGE ... 102

SELF-GOVERNMENT 7
I AM CREATED TO WITNESS ... 128

SELF-GOVERNMENT 8
I AM CREATED TO FORGIVE ... 149

SELF-GOVERNMENT 9
I AM CREATED TO BE HOLY ... 173

SELF-GOVERNMENT 10
I AM CREATED TO WORK ... 197

MUST READ INTRODUCTION: GOD HAS A PLAN

God loves you. He created you. He longs for you to get to know Him better and to walk in His ways. God's love includes a plan for you, your family, the church, and the nation. He fully describes His plan in the Bible.

God's Word warns us about consequences that will occur when a nation turns away from Him. How do you think America is doing? Are we better off today? Are we worse off? The evidence is clear. We are experiencing some of God's consequences right now.

CONSEQUENCES FOR TURNING AWAY FROM GOD AND HIS WORD

- Debt - Deuteronomy 28:44
- More natural disasters – Deuteronomy 28:22-24; 2 Chronicles 7:13
- Losing God's protection – Deuteronomy 28:25
- A far away nation whose language we do not understand will come against us - Deuteronomy 28:49-50

President Andrew Jackson said, **"The Bible is the rock on which our republic rests."** This was true when our nation began, but it is no longer true today.

Today we have removed prayer, the Ten Commandments, and the Bible from our schools. Our families no longer devote time to studying Scripture and to following God's truths and principles.

People believe the lie that the founders wanted a separation of church and state. This lie distorts the meaning of the first amendment. It claims that having God in our schools breaks this amendment. But if this was true, would the authors and founders of the first amendment have had the Bible as the main textbook in their public schools? For four centuries, American families have cherished the Bible. They have believed it to be the rock on which this republic should rest.

In 1647, the first law for public education in America was called, "The Old Deluder Satan Act." The law declared, *"It being one chief project of that old deluder, Satan, to keep men from the knowledge of the Scriptures, as in former time…* Satan's goal is to keep men from the Holy Scriptures because God's Word is what leads people to a saving faith in Christ. Teaching Christianity is the best safeguard for any nation. To remove the teachings of Christ and His Word is to destroy a nation.

Societies of men must be governed in one way or another. They can either be governed with a heavy hand from a civil government or they can be self-governed based upon the teachings of Christ.

Heavy-handed government cannot restrain the sinfulness of man. Christ and Christ alone can change the character of man.

The foundation of Christ and His Word is what keeps a nation free. Do you think our nation is better off after removing God from our public schools? Are we less greedy, violent, or depressed? Are we more financially stable? Are our families more unified and loving or more separated and torn apart? America is suffering because we have taken God out of our lives. We need to repent and accept His perfect plan today.

Our country doesn't have to be this way. We can change the direction of this nation if we repent. Our founders knew this. They stood up and made a declaration to the world that they believed in a Creator. They understood that God had given them unalienable rights to be free and to worship Him as they pleased.

Do you believe the same? Are you willing to stand up for what you believe? Are you willing to cherish the Bible and begin studying it to find out what God's plan is for you, your family, the church, and our nation?

The four books in this series cover God's four ordained institutions: Self-Government / Family Government / Church Government / Civil Government.

They describe ten Life Truths for each institution. Each chapter presents a different Life Truth; a foundation for returning to God and for putting Him and His Word first in your life. Make a commitment to memorize these Life Truths as you work through the chapters.

CONSENT OF THE GOVERNED – ONE FAMILY AT A TIME

Our republic is still based upon the consent of the people. We are a government of the people, by the people, and for the people. As you return to God, and begin fulfilling the purposes God has for you in each of these institutions, seek to recruit others. Pray for our nation. Reach out to others in the hope that God will open their eyes and see the importance of obeying Him.

GOALS TO PRAY FOR:

- Individuals and families to return to studying, memorizing, and obeying God's Word
- Public schools to make the Bible the main textbook again
- The Ten Commandments to be obeyed and taught in our nation

ENGAGE PEOPLE WITH QUESTIONS LIKE THESE:

- Do you know that God has a plan for you, your family, the church, and our nation?
- Do you think our nation is headed in the right direction?
- Do you think our nation is more violent? More greedy?
- Do you think it was a good idea that we removed God and the Ten Commandments from our schools?
- Do you know God's Word says there will be consequences if we turn away from Him? *(Debt, loss of His protection, attacks from a nation from far away whose language we do not understand, more natural disasters)*
- Do you know that God will bless us if we turn back to Him?

FOLLOW UP WITH THIS QUESTION:

- Would you be interested in a Bible Study to learn more about God's plan for you, your family, the church, and our nation?

God allows suffering when we choose to turn away from Him. God promises blessings when we return to Him. Let's return to God and encourage everyone to do the same.

A PLAN OF ACTION FOR YOU, YOUR FAMILY, AND YOUR COMMUNITY:

1. Study and memorize the Life Truths for each institution.
2. Encourage others to join you (door to door, work, family, newspaper, etc…)
3. Encourage others to pray about running for a public office (school board, superintendent, alderman, mayor, etc…)
4. Begin a Facebook page or any other type of social media that will keep people informed (Have your goals clearly marked: We believe in God, the Apostles Creed, the Bible as the rock on which this nation rests, etc…) –This will help alert people to show up at City Hall for a vote or to voice their opinions.
5. Vote for Biblical laws. (Ex: a return to teaching the Bible in public schools)
6. **Direct people to the website *www.bibleistherock.com* for more information.**

A CHALLENGE FOR TODAY

Our founders understood the importance of knowing and heeding God's Word for future posterity. They also understood that godly leaders would need to be trained in the Bible. The first schools in our nation made sure that students got a Biblical education so they could lead with God's Word being the source for all law.

If we are going to have godly laws that lead us in righteousness, then we are going to need men and women who are willing to be the lawmakers. Who do we want in office making the laws that govern our nation? **Men and women who are God-fearing and who know the Bible well.**

For this to happen, "Christian" schools must make it a priority in their curriculum to raise up such leaders and prepare them for public offices. Not only do our "Christian" schools need to step up and refocus some of their goals, but we as a people need to engage more on a local level. We need to be willing to serve as mayors, aldermen, superintendents, and local school board members.

We must return to God so that He can forgive our sin and heal our land. We need to have a confidence and boldness to speak up for what we believe in. We need to study God's Word and teach all who will listen.

If we pray, study God's Word, obey Him, and spread the gospel, then we will be blessed by Him. God will hear our prayers, forgive our sins, and heal America again.

This is not an exhaustive study on the institutions just a starter guide to help us get things back into God's perfect order. *"His will being done on earth as it is in heaven."*

Read all four books and learn God's plan for the institutions.

Book 1 *God has a plan for you*
Self-Government

Book 2 *God has a plan for your family*
Family Government

Book 3 *God has a plan for the church*
Church Government

Book 4 *God has a plan for our nation*
Civil Government

May God bless you and may God bless our nation!

TEN SELF-GOVERNMENT LIFE TRUTHS

1. SCRIPTURE ALONE IS WHAT GOVERNS US

Question: What has God given us to govern our lives by?
Answer: God has given us the Bible to govern our lives by.

2 Timothy 3:16-17 (NIV) [16] All Scripture is God-breathed and is useful for teaching, rebuking, correcting and training in righteousness, [17] so that the man of God may be thoroughly equipped for every good work.

2. WE NEED A NEW NATURE

Question: Where should education begin?
Answer: Education should begin with salvation, because we need a new nature.

Romans 7:18 (NIV) [18] I know that nothing good lives in me, that is, in my sinful nature. For I have the desire to do what is good, but I cannot carry it out.

3. WE MUST CRUCIFY OUR OLD NATURE

Question: What must we do with our old nature?
Answer: We must crucify our old nature and let Christ live through us.

Galatians 2:20 (NIV) [20] *I have been crucified with Christ and I no longer live, but Christ lives in me. The life I live in the body, I live by faith in the Son of God, who loved me and gave himself for me.*

4. I AM CREATED TO SERVE

Question: Does our old nature want to serve others?
Answer: No, it does not. We must crucify our old nature and learn to serve others.

Mark 10:43-44 (NIV) [43] *(Not so with you. Instead), whoever wants to become great among you must be your servant,* [44] *and whoever wants to be first must be slave of all.*

5. I AM CREATED TO PRAISE

Question: Does our old nature want to praise God?
Answer: No, it does not. We must crucify our old nature and praise God.

Colossians 3:16 (NIV) [16] *Let the word of Christ dwell in you richly as you teach and admonish one another with all wisdom, and as you sing psalms, hymns and spiritual songs with gratitude in your hearts to God.*

6. I AM CREATED TO ENCOURAGE

Question: Does our old nature want to encourage others?

Answer: No, it does not. We must crucify our old nature and encourage others.

Hebrews 3:13 (NIV) ¹³ But encourage one another daily, as long as it is called Today, so that none of you may be hardened by sin's deceitfulness.

7. I AM CREATED TO WITNESS

Question: Does our old nature want to witness to others?
Answer: No, it does not. We must crucify our old nature and learn to witness.

Philemon 1:6 (NIV) ⁶ I pray that you may be active in sharing your faith, so that you will have a full understanding of every good thing we have in Christ.

8. I AM CREATED TO FORGIVE

Question: Does our old nature want to forgive to others?
Answer: No, it does not. We must crucify our old nature and learn to forgive.

Matthew 6:14-15 (NIV) ¹⁴ For if you forgive men when they sin against you, your heavenly Father will also forgive you. ¹⁵ But if you do not forgive men their sins, your Father will not forgive your sins.

9. I AM CREATED TO BE HOLY

Question: Does our old nature want to be Holy?
Answer: No, it does not. We must crucify our old nature and learn to be Holy.

I Peter 1:14-15 (NIV) [14] As obedient children, do not conform to the evil desires you had when you lived in ignorance. [15] But just as he who called you is holy, so be holy in all you do;

10. I AM CREATED TO WORK

Question: Does our old nature want to work?
Answer: No, it does not. We must crucify our old nature and learn to work.

I Thessalonians 4:11-12 (NIV) [11] Make it your ambition to lead a quiet life, to mind your own business and to work with your hands, just as we told you, [12] so that your daily life may win the respect of outsiders and so that you will not be dependent on anybody.

SELF-GOVERNMENT
LIFE TRUTH # 1
SCRIPTURE ALONE IS WHAT GOVERNS US

IMPORTANCE OF THE TRUTH

Sola scriptura was the cry of the Protestant Reformation. *Sola scriptura* means that Scripture alone is authoritative for the faith and practice of the Christian life. The Bible is complete, authoritative, and true. It is **ALL** we need to understand God's purpose for our lives and how we are to govern ourselves.

*2 Timothy 3:16 (NIV) ¹⁶ **All** Scripture is God-breathed and is useful for teaching, rebuking, correcting and training in righteousness,*

There are many lies in our generation that seek to discredit the Bible. Here are a few: The Bible was written by man; there are errors in the Bible; it is just another history book.

Here is what the Bible declares. *Psalm 18:30-31 (NIV) ³⁰ As for God, his way is perfect;* **the word of the LORD is flawless**. *He is a shield for all who take refuge in him. ³¹ For who is God besides the LORD? And who is the Rock except our God?*

==We must choose to have faith in God's Word as the ONLY authority that will govern us.==

One of the biggest lies in the last few generations is evolution. Evolution is a lie that seeks to discredit the Scriptures. It states that man came to be from nothing and then evolved into the beings that we are today. Genesis Chapter 1 through Chapter 11 is as true as John 3:16. If the beginning of the Bible is untrue then couldn't it be said that other parts of the Bible are untrue?

==How did Jesus address the book of Genesis?== Jesus talked about Adam and Eve as real people. *Matthew 19:4 (NIV) ⁴ "Haven't you read," he replied, "that at the **beginning the Creator 'made them male and female,'***

Jesus also talked about the flood as a real event. *Luke 17:26-27 (NIV) ²⁶ **"Just as it was in the days of Noah**, so also will it be in the days of the Son of Man. ²⁷ People were eating, drinking, marrying and being given in marriage up to the day Noah entered the ark. Then the flood came and destroyed them all.*

The genealogy of Luke declares Adam to be a real person. *Luke 3:38 (NIV) ³⁸ the son of Enosh, the son of Seth, **the son of Adam**, the son of God.*

==If evolution is true then the Bible is false because it states that in the beginning the Creator made man.== Luke, then, reminds us that the man's name is Adam and traces the genealogy of Jesus to him. **If Adam is not real, then perhaps Jesus is not real.**

As Christians, it is foundational for us to believe what it says in Hebrews 11:3 (NIV) ³ ***By faith*** *we understand that the universe was formed at God's command, so that what is seen was not made out of what was visible.*

Here are a few other beliefs that try to discredit the Bible.

RELATIVISM is the position that all points of view are as valid as any other point of view, and that the individual can decide what is right for himself. Morality could also be dependent upon situations.

If all truth is relative, then the statement "All truth is relative" would be an absolute truth. If it is an absolute truth, then not all things are relative and the statement that "All truth is relative" is false.

If there is no authority or absolute truth, then where can we turn to for TRUTH? What would society look like if every one of us had a different opinion? How could we decide who or what is right? Currently, our society is leaning towards all truth is relative and the Bible is no longer the rock on which our republic resides. This is destroying the God-intended unity that He desires for us to have. We must turn back to the Bible as our standard. Scripture alone is what should govern us.

TOLERANCE – "One of the biggest battles we face concerns the way we use words. One of the most glaring examples is the word 'tolerance'. Not long ago, this meant 'bearing or putting up with someone or something not especially liked'. However, now the word has been redefined to 'all values, all beliefs, all lifestyles, all truth claims are equal'.[1] Denying this makes a person 'intolerant', and thus worthy of contempt." - Jonathan Sarfati

Jesus is forgiving, loving, kind, merciful, and exclusive; but, he would be called intolerant in this generation.

John 14:6 (NIV) [6] ***Jesus answered, "I am the way and the truth and the life. No one comes to the Father except through me."*** Jesus denies any other way to heaven. He claims to be the only way to heaven and the only truth. His teachings are exclusive. Tolerance, as defined in this generation, is false according to the Scriptures.

WHAT DOES THE BIBLE SAY ABOUT MAN DECIDING FOR HIMSELF WHAT IS RIGHT OR WRONG?

1. We can deceive ourselves and therefore we should not be deciding morality.
Proverbs 14:12; 16:25 (NIV) [12] *There is a way that* **seems right** *to a man, but in the end it* **leads to death**.

Proverbs 30:11-12 (NIV) [11] *"There are those who curse their fathers and do not bless their mothers;* [12] ***those*** *who are pure in their own eyes and yet are not cleansed of their filth;*

2. Our desires, likes, or interests cannot be considered morality. (We have desires to do things that the Bible calls sinful.)
*1 Peter 2:11 (NIV) 11 Dear friends, I urge you, as aliens and strangers in the world, to **abstain from sinful desires, which war against your soul**.*

How can we decide what desires are sinful or not? If they are desires, we are going to want to do them, **wanting to do something cannot be the standard for morality. We all have sinful desires and therefore we cannot trust ourselves to produce the standard of morality.** God's Word must be our standard!

THE BIBLE DECLARES THAT IT IS THE ONLY AUTHORITY. THE WORD IS ABSOLUTE TRUTH.

*2 Samuel 22:31 (NIV) 31 "As for God, his way is perfect; **the word of the LORD is flawless.** He is a shield for all who take refuge in him."*

*Psalm 18:30 (NIV) 30 "As for God, his way is perfect; **the word of the LORD is flawless.** He is a shield for all who take refuge in him."*

Isaiah 45:19 (NIV) 19 "I have not spoken in secret, from somewhere in a land of darkness; I have not said to

Jacob's descendants, 'Seek me in vain.' **I, the LORD, speak the truth; I declare what is right."**

Psalm 19:7-8 (NIV) **⁷ *The law of the LORD is perfect, reviving the soul. The statutes of the LORD are trustworthy, making wise the simple.* ⁸ *The precepts of the LORD are right, giving joy to the heart. The commands of the LORD are radiant, giving light to the eyes."***

Jesus said, **"I tell you the truth"** over 30 times in the book of Matthew. (5:18,26; 6:2,5,16; 8:10; 10:15,23,42; 11:11,13,17; 16:28; 17:20; 18:3,13,18; 19:23,28; 21:21,31; 23:36; 24:2,34,47: 25:12,40,45: 26:13,21,24)

OUR CURRENT SOCIETY, EVEN IN THE CHURCH, LOOKS MORE LIKE DEATH THAN LIFE. WHY?

The opposite of life is death. To draw analogies of life we would say that a person is joyful, peaceful, patient, thankful, or we could use the term, "they are full of life." Death, on the other hand, has come to be compared to depression, darkness, sadness, bitterness, confusion, or frustration. You might even say, "That person looks half-dead."

The church is to be the salt of the earth. We are to be the preservers of truth, righteousness, and joy in the Holy Spirit. Unfortunately, the church of today looks more like death. We are in depression, our marriages are falling apart, are children are disrespectful, and we are empty because the world cannot fulfill us. Why does the church of today look more like death? We have forgotten what the Lord said would fulfill us. *Matthew 4:4 (NIV) ⁴ Jesus answered, "It is written: 'Man does not live on bread alone, but on every word that comes from the mouth of God.'"* We must turn back to knowing and doing God's Word.

Jeremiah 7:28 (NIV) ²⁸ Therefore say to them, 'This is the nation that has not obeyed the LORD its God or responded to correction. **Truth has perished; it has vanished from their lips.**

Jeremiah 9:5 (NIV) ⁵ Friend deceives friend, and **no one speaks the truth**. *They have taught their tongues to lie; they weary themselves with sinning.*

Daniel 9:13 (NIV) ¹³ Just as it is written in the Law of Moses, **all this disaster has come upon us, yet we have not sought the favor of the LORD our God by turning from our sins and giving attention to your truth.**

IT IS TIME FOR US TO RETURN TO THE WORD OF GOD AS OUR ONLY SOURCE FOR TRUTH.

Psalm 119:30 (NIV) ³⁰ **I have chosen the way of truth; I have set my heart on your laws.**

John 18:36-37 (NIV) ³⁷ "You are a king, then!" said Pilate. Jesus answered, "You are right in saying I am a king. In fact, for this reason I was born, and for this I came into the world, to testify to the truth. Everyone on the side of truth listens to me."

SINCE THE BIBLE IS WHAT GOVERNS US, HOW OFTEN DOES IT TELL US TO BE IN THE WORD?

*Joshua 1:8 (NIV) ⁸ **Do not let this Book of the Law depart from your mouth; meditate on it day and night, so that you may be careful to do everything written in it. Then you will be prosperous and successful.***

*Psalm 1:1-2 (NIV) ¹ Blessed is the man who does not walk in the counsel of the wicked or stand in the way of sinners or sit in the seat of mockers. ² **But his delight is in the law of the LORD, and on his law he meditates day and night.***

We are to be in the Word every day. To meditate is to ponder the meaning and then apply the meaning to our lives. If we are to ponder on the phrase, "he meditates day and night", we should ask ourselves, "Am I in the Word day and night? Do I concentrate upon God's Word on a daily basis?"

If the answer is no, then we must repent. This is an issue of self-government. God has specifically told us, "blessed is the man", this is a self-government issue;

an area that he wants us to focus on. **God requires us to be meditating upon His Word daily**. We nourish ourselves daily with food, should we not then, nourish ourselves daily with God's truth?

SINCE THE BIBLE IS WHAT GOVERNS US WE MUST MOVE AWAY FROM OUR OPINIONS.

Our society and our families can no longer be built upon our opinions or even parents' opinions. **We must turn to the Scriptures as our ONLY authority to govern us**. As we teach others, we must use the Scriptures and be able to show people specific verses to put the authority back where it belongs. The authority must come from God's Word as we seek to build our lives upon His principles.

I Corinthians 4:6 (NIV) [6] Now, brothers, I have applied these things to myself and Apollos for your benefit, so that you may learn from us the meaning of the saying, **"Do not go beyond what is written."**

*I Corinthians 15:3-4 (NIV) [3] For what I received I passed on to you as of first importance: that Christ died for our sins **according to the Scriptures**, [4] that he was buried, that he was raised on the third day **according to the Scriptures**,*

We must return to God, by submitting to His Word as the **ONLY** authority that will govern us.

As individuals and families we must make this our mission statement: Scripture alone is what governs us. We must begin to read it daily, as he expects of us, and apply the truths that we learn to our lives, in order to bring glory to the One who has created us!

The LIFE TRUTH verse will be ***2 Timothy 3:16-17 (NIV) ¹⁶ All Scripture is God-breathed and is useful for teaching, rebuking, correcting and training in righteousness, ¹⁷ so that the man of God may be thoroughly equipped for every good work.***

If we begin to meditate upon and break the verse down it reveals to us the importance of God's Word in our lives.

All Scripture is God-breathed. (Spoken directly from God to man as 2 Peter 1:21 says)
All Scripture is useful. If it is useful, how often are we using it?

We are to use the Scriptures to teach, rebuke, correct, and train. Are we fulfilling the self-government expectation of using God's Word?

When we teach our children "do not steal", do we show them the verse from the Bible?

The Scriptures are the authority. When we use them as God's Word says we should, we put all authority back where it belongs. It is no longer because you or I said so, but because God said so. Christians are to be the people of the Word, meaning that we have specific verses that govern our lives. We do not steal because God's Word tells us not to in Exodus 20:15. This book will help you find specific verses to govern your life by and to help you teach, rebuke, correct, and train others in righteousness. If we will use the Scriptures like we are told, we will be thoroughly equipped for every good work.

WORKSHEET FOR SELF-GOVERNMENT
LIFE TRUTH # 1
SCRIPTURE ALONE IS WHAT GOVERNS US

Question: What has God given us to govern our lives by?

Answer: God has given us the Bible to govern our lives by.

2 Timothy 3:16-17 (NIV) [16] All Scripture is God-breathed and is useful for teaching, rebuking, correcting and training in righteousness, [17] so that the man of God may be thoroughly equipped for every good work.

> Write out the truth, question, answer and verse on an index card and keep it in your Bible for the week. Work on it every day individually and as a family. Have it memorized by the end of the week.

Read 2 Timothy 3:12-17 and answer the following questions:

The Bible does **not** say that everyone who calls themselves a Christian will be persecuted. Who does it say will be persecuted?

_____

_____

What is the difference between someone who calls themselves a Christian and someone who lives a godly life?

If we stand up and declare that we believe the Bible to be the only source that should govern us, we will be going against the *"evil men and imposters"* of this generation and we will be
P_____.

What is able to make us wise for salvation through faith in Christ Jesus?

How much of the Bible is "God-breathed"?

Fill in the blanks with the four things from verse 16 that explain to us how we can be thoroughly equipped? We need to know God's Word and be able to T_____ our families and those around us.

Beliefs and actions that go against the bible are to be confronted and addressed with Scripture. This is called a R_____. Since we can be deceived, we may need to be C_____ in righteousness. We are all sinners and we have to T_____ ourselves to walk in biblical truth.

In verse 15, we read that Timothy was taught the Holy Scriptures from infancy. Read 2 Tim. 1:5 and Acts 16:1-3, write down who was teaching Timothy? According to these two verses: Joshua 1:8 and Psalm 1:1-2, how often are we to be in the Word?

Question: What has God given us to _____ our lives by?

Answer:

_____

_____.

Based on this LIFE TRUTH what commitments do you need to make to the Bible individually or as a family? How should you go about making decisions? Write out a few commitments that you will make individually and /or as a family.

SELF-GOVERNMENT LIFE TRUTH # 2 – WE NEED A NEW NATURE

THE IMPORTANCE OF THIS TRUTH IS BROKEN DOWN INTO TWO POINTS

1. OUR NATURE BECAME CORRUPTED THROUGH ADAM

When God made Adam and Eve, in the Garden of Eden, he stated that all of His creation was "very good" (Gen 1:31), so how can humans now be considered corrupt? When Adam and Eve ate the forbidden fruit they sinned against God and corrupted their nature. Every human being from Adam on is corrupted in their nature. We have no desire to seek God, love Him, or obey Him. Our very nature is sinful which causes us to sin. Our corrupt and sinful nature produces death in us and harms others around us. *1 Corinthians 15:22 (NIV) [22] For as in Adam all die.* Through Adam we have all become corrupted.

To be depraved is to be corrupted. To be totally depraved means that there is nothing good that lives in any man. As the apostle Paul states, *"[18] I know that nothing good lives in me, that is, in my sinful nature. For I have the desire to do what is good, but I cannot carry it out." Romans 7:18 (NIV)*

This is why Jesus, being born of a virgin, is an important truth of the church today. Christ was not born with the corrupted nature that we received from the beginning with Adam. Jesus was completely sinless, incapable of sin due to the fact that he did not inherit a corrupted nature. (Matt 1:18, 23)

So what is this corrupt nature that I have inherited? Romans 8:7 (NIV) *⁷ the sinful mind is hostile to God. It does not submit to God's law, <u>nor can it do so</u>. ⁸ Those controlled by the sinful nature cannot please God.* Our very nature is to rebel against God. Without a new nature we are like apple trees trying to produce bananas. We cannot.

The understanding of this truth affects the way in which we educate, discipline, pray for the lost, witness, and understand salvation. It affects the way we look at ourselves and deal with the sin issues of our day. Why are there school shootings and other such tragedies in life? Is it mental illness or could it be our corrupted nature? We are all just as guilty as the next person; the only difference may be with the intensity of the evil that comes out of us. One man may physically murder or harm another, while another man hates someone in their hearts. In both cases, the Bible declares these men to be totally depraved before God, both deserving the just penalty of separation from God for eternity in hell.

Matthew 5:21-22 (NIV) ²¹ "You have heard that it was said to the people long ago, 'Do not murder, and anyone who murders will be subject to judgment.' ²² But I tell you that anyone who is angry with his brother will be subject to judgment. Again, anyone who says to his brother, 'Raca,' is answerable to the Sanhedrin. But anyone who says, 'You fool!' will be in danger of the fire of hell. (Note: I am not saying there are no mental illnesses; but I am saying that many times we label corrupt nature as mental illness.)

A just God cannot overlook a lawbreaker. We understand this point from how we handle lawbreakers in our own society. If a man commits a terrible, senseless murder, we know that he needs to be brought to justice and then punished for his actions. God's punishment for sin is death.

Ezekiel 18:20 (NIV) ²⁰ The soul who sins is the one who will die. The son will not share the guilt of the father, nor will the father share the guilt of the son. The righteousness of the righteous man will be credited to him, and the wickedness of the wicked will be charged against him.

James 2:10 (NIV) ¹⁰ For whoever keeps the whole law and yet stumbles at just one point is guilty of breaking all of it.

This Biblical truth goes against the teachings of this generation in which many believe that all men are inherently "good" and we just need to bring the "good" out of ourselves.

Mark 10:18 (NIV) ¹⁸ *Jesus answered.* **"No one is good-- except God alone**. This teaching that we have "good" within us is contrary to the Scriptures.

Romans 3:10-11 (NIV) ¹⁰ *As it is written: "There is* **no one** *righteous,* **not even one**; ¹¹ *there is* **no one** *who understands,* **no one** *who seeks God.*

This teaching does not mean that man cannot do anything "good" in the eyes of man, or that we are all intense sinners. It does say that we are all in the same boat together and the boat is called depravity. We are all corrupted by sin, from Adam's original sin in the garden, to our own sin that we commit against God.

God in His mercy and love for us gave us the law (Ten Commandments) to reveal to us just what kind of sinners we really are.

Romans 3:19-20 (NIV) ¹⁹ *Now we know that whatever the law says, it says to those who are under the law, so that* **every mouth may be silenced and the whole world held accountable to God.** ²⁰ *Therefore* **no one** *will be declared righteous in his sight by observing the law; rather,* **through the law we become conscious of sin.**

God gave us the Ten Commandments that we are to obey, but also to reveal to us that we have a corrupt nature that does not want to Love God or His ways.

Have you ever lied? Yes, we all have – **GUILTY**
Have you ever not honored your mother and father? Yes, we all have – **GUILTY**
Have you ever not honored the Sabbath? Yes, we all have – **GUILTY**
Have you ever loved something more than God (idolatry)? Yes, we all have - **GUILTY**

Romans 3:19 declares that all of our mouths are silenced when we look at ourselves according to God's righteous standards. Then, verse 20 tells us that the law reveals to us our sin and our sinful state. The apostle Paul writes in *Romans 7:24 (NIV) [24] What a wretched man I am! Who will rescue me from this body of death?*

So how wretched are we? We are totally depraved and we are completely and utterly unable to do anything about our condition. Unfortunately, in our state of corruption, many times we do not even see our state before God. We compare ourselves to others. We look at only the "good" things that we do. We continually justify ourselves before a holy God. But this is how God sees us:

Revelation 3:17-18 (NIV) [17] You say, 'I am rich; I have acquired wealth and do not need a thing.' But you do not realize that you are **wretched, pitiful, poor, blind and naked**. *[18] I counsel you to buy from me gold refined in the fire, so you can become rich; and white clothes to wear, so you can cover your shameful nakedness; and salve to put on your eyes, so you can see.*

Since Scripture alone is what governs, let's look at three ways the Bible describes our state.

a. Without Christ we are bound for hell

Galatians 3:22 (NIV) ²² But the Scripture declares that the whole world is a prisoner of sin, The Bible declares that all of us, because of our sin, has made us prisoners of sin. Since, God is holy and cannot be around sin we are bound for hell.

Are we really that corrupted and evil that we would be bound for hell? Yes! Have you ever been in a situation where you lost your temper and evil started coming out of your mouth? You said hateful and hurtful words. Have you ever regretted what you said and even wondered where that came from? It comes from our sinful nature which is corrupt.

James 3:6 (NIV) ⁶ The tongue also is a fire, a world of evil among the parts of the body. It corrupts the whole person, sets the whole course of his life on fire, and is itself set on fire by hell.

b. We can be blinded about our own condition

2 Corinthians 4:4 (NIV) *⁴ The god of this age (Satan) has blinded the minds of unbelievers, so that they cannot see the light of the gospel of the glory of Christ, who is the image of God.* John 12:40 is a similar verse that speaks about how blind we are in our sin. We can justify

ourselves and feel secure in our corruption, but we are deceived. If we do not understand our corrupt selfish nature we will end up in hell. Our flaws and the fact that we continue to do the very things that we say we will never do again should reveal to us our corruption.

c. Satan wants to destroy our lives and the lives around us

*1 John 5:19 (NIV) ¹⁹ We know that we are children of God, and that the **whole world is under the control of the evil one.***

*Ephesians 2:1-3 (NIV) ¹ As for you, you were **dead in your transgressions and sins,** ² in which you used to live when you followed the ways of this world and of the ruler of the kingdom of the air, **the spirit who is now at work in those who are disobedient.** ³ All of us also lived among them at one time, gratifying the cravings of our sinful nature and following its desires and thoughts. Like the rest, **we were by nature objects of wrath.***

When we sin, we become a slave to sin, and give control of our lives to Satan. We think that we are in control, but the Bible declares that there are only two powers and we are not one of them. You are either under the control and influence of Satan or you are under the power of the Holy Spirit. The scary thing is that we can be destroying many lives and not even realizing it. A man who does not bring his family up in the training and instruction of the

Lord is just as much a destroyer of lives as the man who enters into a room and kills people. The man who does not obey God's command to teach the Word to his children is not only deceiving and destroying their lives but he is destroying the next generation.

Look at our society today. Look at our government and the tragedies that are going on almost daily. Where is it originating? Did these children grow up knowing that they have a sinful nature and are in need of Jesus to give them a new nature? Were they taught the Word and the dangers of following their own evil desires? There is no God in our government because we have a generation of people who have grown up without being taught scripture, God's Holy Word.

1 Peter 5:8 (NIV) [8] Be self-controlled and alert. Your enemy the devil prowls around like a roaring lion looking for someone to devour.

Again, the apostle Paul writes in *Romans 7:24, (NIV) [24] What a wretched man I am! Who will rescue me from this body of death? This brings us to our second point which also brings us the good news!*

2. THROUGH JESUS WE CAN HAVE A NEW NATURE

*Who can rescue us? Romans 7:25 (NIV) *²⁵* Thanks be to God–through Jesus Christ our Lord!* He can rescue us from our totally depraved state.

What good would it be for a man to live his life acquiring wealth, property, friends, respect, admiration, plus lots of entertainment and leisure? Sounds like the perfect life, doesn't it? Who wouldn't want to have all of those things? On the surface, the question may seem odd, but with God's perspective those "things" the man acquired will fade away as dust in the wind.

Look at how Jesus put it *Matthew 16:26 (NIV) *²⁶* What good will it be for a man if he gains the whole world, yet forfeits his soul? Or what can a man give in exchange for his soul?*

If we live our lives thinking that we are pleasing to God, and that we are doing enough "good" to appease the wrath of God from falling upon us, we are deceived. When our life is over and we are standing before God, none of these "things" that we have acquired will amount to anything. Could we offer God money to enter into heaven? Could we claim our good deeds and how we helped others? Could we ask him to call our friends and have them put in a good word in for us? The deeper question is, are we living our lives for ourselves, or are we living our lives to glorify God? Selfish ambition is a flaw in our nature that will cause us to be separated from God forever. Galatians 5:20, lists sins that if we live in them, will keep us from entering into the Kingdom of Heaven. Selfish ambition is one of those sins. We cannot live to please ourselves; we must live to please God.

Justice must be carried out. How could a just God ignore or even excuse our sin? He cannot! He will not! The sentence must be carried out.

Many of us know this passage *John 3:16 (NIV) ¹⁶ "For God so loved the world **that he gave** his one and only Son, that whoever believes in him shall not perish but have eternal life.* I'm not sure that we fully understand what it means when it says, "he gave." He gave Christ? Yes, he gave him to be the substitute for our punishment. Not just any punishment, but God's wrath was poured out on him. Here is how the Bible describes what he gave His son unto:

*Galatians 3:13 (NIV) ¹³ Christ redeemed us from the curse of the law **by becoming a curse for us**, for it is written: "Cursed is everyone who is hung on a tree."*

*I Peter 2:24 (NIV) ²⁴ He himself **bore our sins in his body** on the tree, so that we might die to sins and live for righteousness; by **his wounds** you have been healed.*

*Matthew 27:26-31 (NIV)²⁶ Then he released Barabbas to them. But he **had Jesus flogged (flogging was a*** *brutal beating that was done with many whips on the end of a stick. The strands on the whip had glass and other sharp objects attached so that when they hit a man the straps would wrap around the body and then rip the skin off),* and handed him over to be crucified. ²⁷ Then the governor's soldiers took Jesus into the Praetorium and gathered the whole company of soldiers around him. ²⁸ They **stripped him** and put a scarlet robe on him, ²⁹ and then twisted together a **crown of thorns** and set it on his head. They put a staff in his right hand and knelt in front of him and **mocked him**. "Hail, king of the Jews!" they said. ³⁰ They **spit on him**, and took the staff and **struck him on the head again and again**. ³¹ After they had mocked him, they took off the robe and put his own clothes on him. Then they led him away to **crucify him**.

Just before this brutal treatment of God, Jesus was in the Garden of Gethsemane. He knew the soldiers were on their way to crucify him and he was praying.

Mark 14:36 (NIV) ³⁶ "Abba, Father," he said, *"everything is possible for you. **Take this cup from me**. Yet not what I will, but what you will."* What cup was Jesus referring to? Some scholars believe that he was saying, "Father, please, do not allow me to experience the cup of your wrath." The sins of the whole world were placed upon Jesus and the wrath of God was delivered upon Him to make atonement for our sins.

Jesus took the wrath that I deserved. Jesus took the punishment that I deserved for the evil that I did. For those careless, hurtful words that came forth out of my mouth. For those actions that I now regret and know caused pain to others that I love. My corruption deserved that punishment. If you are honest, you would say that your corruption deserves the wrath of God as well. But not Jesus! He did not deserve any of it!

I John 2:2 (NIV) ² *He is the atoning sacrifice for our sins, and* **not only for ours but also for the sins of the whole world.**

Wow! That is amazing love! So then, are we all saved? Has God taken care of everything and we no longer have to worry about the wrath of God? No, as God enables us to come to Him we still must respond.

John 3:17-18 (NIV) ¹⁷ *For God did not send his Son into the world to condemn the world, but to save the world through him.* ¹⁸ *Whoever believes in him is not condemned, but* **whoever does not believe stands condemned already** *because he has not believed in the name of God's one and only Son.*

When the Holy Spirit awakens us to the truth that we need Jesus, then we must choose to respond. He enables, and then, we must respond.

We are so corrupted that we would never choose to seek God. God's spirit must first enlighten us to our need of Him and then He enables us to respond. *John 6:44 (NIV) ⁴⁴ "**No one can come to me unless the Father who sent me draws him**.*
When God reveals our need and enables us we must still respond. *Matthew 4:17 (NIV) ¹⁷ From that time on Jesus began to preach, "Repent, for the kingdom of heaven is near."*

Has the Holy Spirit revealed to you that you are totally depraved and in need of Jesus? Then do what Peter told the crowd to do when their hearts were awakened to the truth. *Acts 3:19 (NIV) ¹⁹ Repent, then, and turn to God, so that your sins may be wiped out, that times of refreshing may come from the Lord.*

Repentance means to stop living our lives based upon our corrupted minds and opinions and start listening to and obeying the Bible. That is what these LIFE TRUTHS are all about. Submitting to the governing authority of the Word of God and obeying the principles that God has set out for us, by the power of the Holy Spirit within us.

When we repent, God gives us:

a. **A new nature.** *2 Corinthians 5:17 (NIV) ¹⁷ Therefore, if anyone is in Christ, he is a new creation; the old has gone, the new has come!*

b. **A new mind.** *I Corinthians 2:16 (NIV)* *¹⁶ "For who has known the mind of the Lord that he may instruct him?" But we have the mind of Christ.*
  c. **The Holy Spirit.** *Acts 2:38 (NIV) ³⁸ Peter replied, "Repent and be baptized, every one of you, in the name of Jesus Christ for the forgiveness of your sins. And you will receive the gift of the Holy Spirit.*

Why should education begin with salvation? Have you ever met someone who was disrespectful, has no love for God or others, is lazy, a liar, selfish, a complainer, argumentative, materialistic, or just lives for themselves? Should we try to teach that person to be "good" or to be saved? Perhaps, they behave like they do because they do not have a new nature.

When John the Baptist came on the scene to prepare the way for Jesus, what was his message? Did he come saying, "there is good in all of us and we need to just learn to bring it out?" What did he teach to educate us about God? *Matthew 3:1-2 (NIV) ¹ In those days John the Baptist came, preaching in the Desert of Judea ² and saying,* **"Repent,** *for the kingdom of heaven is near."*

Matthew 3:7-10 (NIV) ⁷ But when he saw many of the Pharisees and Sadducees coming to where he was baptizing, he said to them: "You brood of vipers! Who warned you to flee from the coming wrath? ⁸ Produce fruit in keeping with repentance. ⁹ And do not think you can say to yourselves, 'We have Abraham as our father.' I tell you that out of these stones God can raise up children for Abraham. ¹⁰ The ax is already at the root of the trees, and *every tree that does not produce good fruit will be cut down and thrown into the fire.*

John declared a nature change is what can save you from the coming wrath. *"Every tree that does not produce good fruit will be cut down and thrown into the fire."* Then he goes on to say that that the nature change is from the Holy Spirit. *Matthew 3:11 (NIV) [11] "I baptize you with water for repentance. But after me will come one who is more powerful than I, whose sandals I am not fit to carry. He will baptize you with the Holy Spirit and with fire.* **John started his education with the need for a nature change.**

Jesus came and began his teaching ministry and what did he come saying? *Matthew 4:17 (NIV) [17] From that time on Jesus began to preach, "Repent, for the kingdom of heaven is near."*

The fact that we need a new nature should cause us to educate ourselves and others as Jesus did. It should cause us to search the Scriptures and seek to honor Him as His living word is revealed to us. It should cause us to pray more for our loved ones and to be deeply concerned when we do not see the "fruit" of God coming from them. Are their words and their actions as loving as the words and actions of Jesus? There is nothing good that lives in us, that is in our sinful nature. We must proclaim our need for Jesus to a lost and dying world.

WORKSHEET FOR SELF-GOVERNMENT
LIFE TRUTH # 2
WE NEED A NEW NATURE

Question: Where should education begin?
Answer: Education should begin with salvation, because we need a new nature.

> *Romans 7:18 (NIV) ¹⁸ I know that nothing good lives in me, that is, in my sinful nature. For I have the desire to do what is good, but I cannot carry it out.*
>
> Write out the Life Truth, question, and answer on one side of an index card and the verse on the other side. Keep it in your Bible for the week. Work on it every day individually and as a family. Have it memorized by next week.

This passage declares the totally depravity of man. Read Romans 3:10-20 and answer the following questions:
Is there anyone who is righteous?_____ Is there anyone who understands?_____ Is there anyone who seeks God?_____ Is there anyone who fears God?_____

Since we are totally depraved and unable to seek God how can we come to know God and experience His salvation? (Hint John 6:44)

Once God has revealed to us that we are corrupted and in need of His salvation what must we do to be saved according to these verses in the Bible?

Rom 10:9,10 C_____ J_____ Is L_____. B_____ in your H_____. Acts 3:19 R_____. T_____ to God.
In your own words define what repentance is and give an example of it?

When we repent, God gives us:
a. A new nature. *2 Corinthians 5:17 (NIV)*
b. A new _____. The mind of C_____ *1 Corinthians 2:16 (NIV)*
c. The H_____ S_____. *Acts 2:38 (NIV)*

When we are born again and we receive our new nature the old nature is still with us. What is our responsibility to the old nature? *Romans 8:12-14 (NIV)*
If we live according to the sinful N_____ we will D_____. (Refers to spiritual death – hell)
By the S_____ we are to P_____ to D_____ the M_____ of the body.
Then, we will L_____. (Refers to spiritual life – heaven)

Based on this LIFE TRUTH, name one misdeed that needs to be put to death in your old nature and ask God to "by the Spirit" put it to death. (Examples of an area: pride, selfishness, complaining, disrespect, gossip, idleness, arguing, anger, filthy language)

SELF-GOVERNMENT
LIFE TRUTH # 3
WE MUST CRUCIFY OUR OLD NATURE

When God draws us to himself, He enables us to respond to His call by repenting and making Him Lord. If we repent, something awesome happens! We become born again. *John 3:5-6*

To be born again is to receive a new nature, a new mind, and the Holy Spirit. But what happens to our old nature when we receive this new nature? Unfortunately, the old nature is still with us. This is the struggle Christians face until this earthly corrupted nature dies and we are clothed with our heavenly bodies free from corruption. The apostle Paul says it this way in *2 Corinthians 5:2 (NIV)* *² Meanwhile we groan, longing to be clothed with our heavenly dwelling.*

Why would we still groan if we have a new nature? We groan because the old nature still has sinful desires that pull at us and tempt us to do evil. Paul calls this struggle a conflict that is within us.

*Galatians 5:17 (NIV) ¹⁷ For the sinful nature desires what is contrary to the Spirit, and the Spirit what is contrary to the sinful nature. They are in **conflict** with each other, so that you do not do what you want.*

Peter calls this struggle a war as our sinful desires pull at us to disobey God. *I Peter 2:11-12 (NIV) ¹¹ Dear friends, I urge you, as aliens and strangers in the world, to abstain from sinful desires, which **war** against your soul.*

What, then, is our responsibility to the old nature? *2 Corinthians 4:10-11 (NIV) ¹⁰ We always carry around in our body the death of Jesus, so that the life of Jesus may also be revealed in our body. ¹¹ **For we who are alive are always being given over to death for Jesus' sake, so that his life may be revealed in our mortal body.***

In our new nature we are to be denying the old wants, desires, and plans. We must remember that our old ways are corrupt, selfish, and for our own gratification. We are to put the old nature to death in order that the life of Jesus is evident in our lives. Many have heard the phrase, "What would Jesus do?" This phrase is exactly the mindset believers need as they seek to obey God. If Jesus was living His life through me what would He do? How would He respond to the situations that arise in my life? The exciting truth about these questions is that, as Christians, they become a reality in our lives. Jesus' nature and character begin to be displayed through us. Christ's character pouring out of our lives is the evidence that we are born again. When we begin to speak and act like Jesus, then we can be confident that Christ is in us!

God's will for our lives is that we are "*conformed to the likeness of his Son*". *Romans 8:29 (NIV)* In order for this to happen, we must do our part.

Look at what Jesus said in, *Luke 9:23-24 (NIV)* *[23] Then he said to them all: "If anyone would come after me, he must deny himself and take up his cross daily and follow me. [24] For whoever wants to save his life will lose it, but whoever loses his life for me will save it.*

We must deny our wants and desires and make God's wants and desires our priorities. We must take up our cross daily as we seek to crucify our old nature. We must lose our life's ambitions, goals, and dreams to follow Christ and be able to enter into the Kingdom of Heaven.

If you were to die today, would there be enough evidence to convict you of being a Christian? When Jesus spoke about heaven, he called it a Kingdom. In a Kingdom, there is only one ruler and He is Jesus our Lord. We must submit our lives to King Jesus to enter into His Kingdom. This is repentance: when we no longer live for ourselves, but for him who gave his life for us. We live to please him. We understand that he created us to love him and others.

What is the process for crucifying our old nature? How do we go about it? Where do we start?
In preparing the way for Christ, John taught the people, *Luke 3:7-9 (NIV)* *[7] John said to the crowds*

coming out to be baptized by him, "You brood of vipers! Who warned you to flee from the coming wrath? [8] Produce fruit in keeping with repentance. And do not begin to say to yourselves, 'We have Abraham as our father.' For I tell you that out of these stones God can raise up children for Abraham. [9] The ax is already at the root of the trees, and every tree that does not produce good fruit will be cut down and thrown into the fire."

The coming wrath will be poured out on the disobedient and unrepentant. (Roman 1:18; 2:5; Colossians 3:6) John tells us to produce fruit in keeping with repentance. Crucifying our flesh is a process and Paul tells us in Romans that we have an obligation to "put to death the misdeeds of the body".

Since Scripture alone is what governs us, what does the Bible say about crucifying our sinful nature? Most of us know what we need to be working on, but sometimes we need to ask God to reveal deeper things that we need to work on. Deeper issues would include things like the motives of our heart, un-forgiveness, and pride.

HERE ARE THREE THINGS THAT WE CAN DO TO HELP CRUCIFY OUR OLD NATURE

1. ASK GOD FOR AREAS TO WORK ON. Ask God to reveal to you areas that you need to put to death. *Psalm 139:23-24 (NIV) [23] Search*

me, O God, and know my heart; test me and know my anxious thoughts. [24] See if there is any offensive way in me, and lead me in the way everlasting. This is vital since we have already learned that we can be deceived, and blinded to the things of God. We love to justify ourselves and think that we are looking good to man but underneath we could be full of greed or selfish envy. In sincerity, ask God to reveal to you any sinful motives or character flaws that need to be dealt with.

2. MEMORIZE SCRIPTURE. Scripture Memory is vital to putting to death our old nature. *Psalm 119:11 (NIV) I have hidden your word in my heart that I might not sin against you.*

    If we really want to know God and find out what pleases Him we are going to be searching His Word. As our Self-Government LIFE TRUTH number one tells us, "All Scripture" is what God has given us to govern our lives by. If you have no desire to read the Word, it can only be one of two things: You either do not have a new nature that would draw you to His Word or you are allowing your old nature to keep you out of the Word. There is a verse in the Bible to deal with every old nature issue that you could be going through. In your new nature you should search the Scriptures to find a verse that relates to the issue that you are seeking to put to death. Memorize the passage and let God's Word begin to defeat your old nature. In many cases there are several verses that you could memorize to defeat your sin nature.

Psalm 119:11 is not only about defeating sin in our lives but preparing ourselves not to sin. Many Christians go out into the world with no Scriptural foundation. When the cares of this life come, they fall into sin, mainly, because they do not know the Holy Scriptures. How many young people have married a non-Christian, suffered in their marriage, and eventually ended up divorced? The Scriptures are clear that we should not be yoked with an unbeliever (2 Corinthians 6:14). If this Life Truth was memorized and meditated upon, young people who desire to honor God with their lives would avoid this area of sin. As Christians, we have the responsibility to train up our children and prepare them to live holy and righteous lives. Scripture memory is vital in this process. These Life Truths are just a beginning in the process of teaching our children in the way that they should go (Proverbs 22:6).

3. **MEDITATE UPON GOD'S WORD.** Meditate on the passages you are memorizing and the

Word of God. *Psalm 119:97 (NIV) ⁹⁷ Oh, how I love your law! I meditate on it all day long.*

What we meditate upon affects us greatly. *Proverbs 24:2 (NIV) ² for their hearts plot violence, and their lips talk about making trouble.* The old nature focuses on selfish things and in the heart we meditate upon our sin and then our sin comes to fruition. The wicked man meditates upon and talks about violence and then it comes out of him. The righteous meditate upon God's Word and talk about God's Word and then righteousness comes out. As James tells us in *James 1:25 (NIV) ²⁵ But the man who looks intently into the **perfect law** (God's Word) that gives freedom, and continues to do this, not forgetting what he has heard, but doing it—he will be blessed in what he does.*

THERE ARE TWO MOTIVATIONS TO PUTTING THE OLD NATURE TO DEATH

1. Fear of the Lord

The Bible says, "**The fear of the LORD is the beginning of wisdom**; all who follow his precepts have good understanding. To him belongs eternal praise" Psalm 111:10 (NIV).
It also says in *Proverbs 16:6 (NIV) ⁶ Through love and faithfulness sin is atoned for;* **through the fear of the LORD a man avoids evil.**

Paul wrote in 2 Corinthians 5:11 (NIV) **¹¹ Since, then, we know what it is to fear the Lord,** *we try to persuade men.*

What is it to fear the Lord? How will that help us put to death our old nature? Just prior to that verse is the importance of fearing the Lord.

2 Corinthians 5:9-10 (NIV) ⁹ So we make it our goal to please him, whether we are at home in the body or away from it. **¹⁰ For we must all appear before the judgment seat of Christ.**

The crucial weight is in the fact that we will all appear before the judgment seat of Christ to receive what is due us. The good and the bad that we do here on the earth will be brought to the judgment and we will stand trial for it.

The Bible gives us some insight into the judgment and some of the things that we will be held accountable for.

    a. **OUR WORDS** - *Matthew 12:36-37 (NIV) ³⁶ But I tell you that men will have to give account on the day of judgment for every careless word they have spoken. ³⁷ For by your words you will be acquitted, and by your words you will be condemned."*

    b. **OUR DEEDS** - *2 Corinthians 5:10 (NIV) ¹⁰ For we must all appear before the judgment* *seat of Christ, that each one may receive what is due him for <u>the things done</u> while in the body, whether good or bad.*

Paul was witnessing to Governor Felix and teaching him about faith in Christ. Look at what he said in *Acts 24:24-25 (NIV) 24 Several days later Felix came with his wife Drusilla, who was a Jewess. He sent for Paul and listened to him as he spoke about faith in Christ Jesus. 25 As Paul discoursed on righteousness, self-control and the judgment to come, Felix was afraid and said, "That's enough for now! You may leave. When I find it convenient, I will send for you."*

Why was Felix afraid? He was afraid because of the fear of the judgment. **We must display self-control and righteousness which is impossible to do without Christ in us.** Even when we receive our new nature we still have the responsibility to crucify our old self.

Have you ever really contemplated the judgment? We will stand trial on what basis? What charges will be presented for my conviction or my acquittal? The key is not to look around you at all the other people headed to trial and compare yourself to them. The charge, as we learned in our Life Truth number two is that we all have a corrupted nature and we all stand guilty before a Holy God. We are all in the same boat of the condemned. So what is the judgment? The judgment will be based upon the evidence. What evidence is there that Christ is in you? Is your old flesh dying? Can we see Jesus in you? His words, His love, His mercy, His actions?

Paul said it this way, *Galatians 2:20 (NIV) [20] I have been crucified with Christ and I no longer live, but Christ lives in me. The life I live in the body, I live by faith in the Son of God, who loved me and gave himself for me.*

In the book of Acts, we read that the gospel reached Antioch and a great number of the people believed. The church in Jerusalem heard about this and they sent Barnabas to check it out. The Bible says, *Acts 11:23 (NIV) [23] When he arrived and saw the* **evidence** *of the grace of God, he was glad and encouraged them all to remain true to the Lord with all their hearts.*

This is also the first place that people were called Christians. The very word Christian means like Christ. Barnabas saw the evidence that these people had a new nature. He saw Jesus in them. Is there enough evidence to convict you as a Christian? Notice I did not say a religious person, because today a person can be called a "Christian" and yet live a lifestyle that doesn't reflect Christ. Homosexuality, sexual immorality, *the cravings of sinful man, the lust of the eyes and the boasting of what he says and does—comes not from the Father but from the world.* I John 2:16. These characteristics are not Christ-like and reveal a lack of evidence that Christ is in you. Again, on the Day of Judgment will there be enough evidence to convict you of being Christ-like?

Some might say that we are saved by grace and not by works, and that this sounds like a "works" salvation. **I am not promoting a works salvation, but Biblical salvation.** The works are not from us but from the very fact that Christ is in us. We are to be no longer living but Christ is to be living in and through us. Listen to what James said, *James 2:20 (NIV) [20] You foolish man, do you want **evidence** that faith without deeds is useless?* We are all corrupted and sinful and when we become born again Christ begins to live His life through us.

Ephesians 2:8-10 (NIV) [8] For it is by grace you have been saved, through faith–and this not from yourselves, it is the gift of God– [9] not by works, so that no one can boast. [10] For we are God's workmanship, **created in Christ Jesus to do good works, which God prepared in advance for us to do.**

We are to display God's works or as Jesus taught, the fruit or evidence should come out of us. Paul declared in Galatians that "he no longer lived but that Christ lived in Him,"

Galatians 2:21 (NIV) [21] I do not set aside the grace of God, for if righteousness could be gained through the law, Christ died for nothing!"

It is Christ in us enabling us to live holy and righteous lives. If there is no evidence of that in your life, then you should be very concerned about the Day of Judgment.

What happens if we receive our new nature and decide not to deny our old sinful desires? What happens if we refuse to walk by the Spirit and we choose to go our own way? *Hebrews 10:26-27 (NIV) [26] If we deliberately keep on sinning after we have received the knowledge of the truth, no sacrifice for sins is left, [27] but only a fearful expectation of judgment and of raging fire that will consume the enemies of God.* Hell is going to be a terrible punishment and unimaginable suffering, but the Bible talks about an even worse punishment. In fact, it states that those who know better will have a worse punishment than those who did not. This means that those who understand the gospel, who understand their need to be crucifying the flesh and living to please God but still refuse, will receive a worse punishment than the lost. (Luke 12:48)

The fear of God should compel us to be holy as God has called us to be. *Romans 2:5-8 (NIV) [5] But because of your stubbornness and your unrepentant heart, you are storing up wrath against yourself for the day of God's wrath, when his righteous judgment will be revealed. [6] God "will give to each person according to what he has done." [7] To those who by persistence in doing good seek glory, honor and immortality, he will give eternal life. [8] But for those who are self-seeking and who reject the truth and follow evil, there will be wrath and anger.*

If you have no desire to make Christ's desires yours, or you have no desire to read the Word, or you have no desire to pray and seek God, then there is a very good chance that you do not have a new nature. If you do not have a new nature, you are not born again; and if you are not born again, you are not saved. This should greatly concern us in our own lives and the lives of those around us. Do we see evidence in our children's lives that they have a new nature and want to honor God? Do we see evidence in our friends and families lives that they have a new nature which is causing them to become more like Christ? We must pray and seek to persuade everyone to come to know Christ as their Lord for their salvation.

2. Christ Love compels us

Okay, so fear compels us because we need to be concerned about the judgment, but does love compel us as well? How can fear and love compel us? Paul writes in *2 Corinthians 5:14-15 (NIV) ¹⁴ For Christ's love compels us, because we are convinced that one died for all, and therefore all died. ¹⁵ And he died for all, that those who live should no longer live for themselves but for him who died for them and was raised again.*

When we reflect upon what Christ did for us and the great suffering that he endured on our behalf it causes us to be compelled to honor Him with our lives. The God of the universe came down from His throne in heaven and he died on the cross for me. Not because I deserved for Him to do it, but because he loved me and He did not want to spend an eternity without me. He wants to have a relationship with me. Wow, me a wretched sinner. As the verse states, *"we are convinced that one (Jesus) died for all"* and that "all" includes me. Christ died for me and He died for you. A God that would die for us, so that we do not have to spend an eternity in hell, this kind of love should compel us to "no longer live for ourselves" but to live for Jesus.

This kind of love should compel us to please him and be like Him in this world. We are careful about what we say and do, because we seek to glorify the God who loved us enough to redeem us from hell and our corrupted state. The fear of judgment begins our path of putting to death our old nature. But as we experience more and more of the love of God, his unfailing love drives out the fear of punishment, knowing that Christ is in us, the hope of glory.

I John 4:16-18 (NIV) ¹⁶ And so we know and rely on the love God has for us. God is love. Whoever lives in love lives in God, and God in him. ¹⁷ <u>In this way, love is made complete among us so that we will have confidence on the day of judgment,</u> **because in this world we are like him.** *¹⁸ There is no fear in love. But perfect love drives out fear, because fear has to do with punishment. The one who fears is not made perfect in love.*

Are you afraid of the judgment? Does it concern you to stand before God to be judged according to your words, actions, and even the very motives of your heart? Then cry out as the repentant tax collector did in *Luke 18:9-14 (NIV) ⁹ To some who were confident of their own righteousness and looked down on everybody else, Jesus told this parable: [10] "Two men went up to the temple to pray, one a Pharisee and the other a tax collector. [11] The Pharisee stood up and prayed about himself: 'God, I thank you that I am not like other men—robbers, evildoers, adulterers—or even like this tax collector. [12] I fast twice a week and give a tenth of all I get.' [13] "But the tax collector stood at a distance. He would not even look up to heaven, but beat his breast and said, 'God, have mercy on me, a sinner.' [14] "I tell you that this man, rather than the other, went home justified before God. For everyone who exalts himself will be humbled, and he who humbles himself will be exalted."*

Oh, that we would see our corrupted nature and we would cry out to God for mercy. That we would lay our selfish ambition, pride, justifications, self-righteousness, and be justified by the one who can save us. That we would experience His great love for us, and that it would compel us to deny ourselves, pick up our crosses, and follow Him.

WORKSHEET FOR SELF-GOVERNMENT
LIFE TRUTH # 3
WE MUST CRUCIFY OUR OLD NATURE

Question: What must we do with our old nature?
Answer: We must crucify our old nature and let Christ live through us.

> *Galatians 2:20 (NIV) [20] I have been crucified with Christ and I no longer live, but Christ lives in me. The life I live in the body, I live by faith in the Son of God, who loved me and gave himself for me.*
>
> Write out the Life Truth, question, and answer on one side of an index card and the verse on the other side. Keep it in your Bible for the week. Work on it every day individually and as a family. Have it memorized by next week.

Read Ephesians 4:17-24 and answer the following questions:
Many of the people in the Ephesian church were Gentiles, so why was Paul telling them not to live like the Gentiles?

Paul uses words and phrases like futile, darkened in their understanding, ignorant, and hard hearts. Do you think the non-Christian Gentiles felt this way about themselves? Why or Why not?

What could it reveal about a person who does not want to obey God's Word by coming out of the world, putting their old self to death, and living in true righteousness and holiness? (Hint Matt 7:16-18)

The Bible says, *"that we will all appear before the judgment seat of Christ"* What do you think we will be judged for according to these verses?
OUR W_____ - *Matthew 12:36-37;* OUR
D_____ - *2 Corinthians 5:10*
OUR T_____ - *2 Corinthians 10:5;* OUR
H_____ - *Hebrews 3:12*

What does this verse tell us we need to do to crucify our old nature? (Psalm 119:11)

In Acts 11:23 and in 2 Thessalonians 1:5 it talks about the evidence that Christ is in us. In Acts, they are called Christians there first. What kind of evidence did Barnabas most likely see when he met these believers? (Example: Their Love)

In Thessalonians Paul commends them for their growing faith and love as evidence, but he also boasts about their perseverance in persecutions and trials that they were enduring. Enduring for Christ is evidence that Christ is in us. What kinds of persecutions, trials, or sufferings might a Christian go through today?

Based on this LIFE TRUTH, and in view of the judgment, what area(s) do you need to be working on to continue crucifying your old nature? On the day of judgment will there be enough evidence that Christ is in you to convict you? (Your character and sufferings)

SELF-GOVERNMENT
LIFE TRUTH # 4
I AM CREATED TO SERVE

In our new nature we need to understand that we are created to serve. We must learn to serve because our old nature has a self-centered desire to be served. The opposite of servant-hood is selfishness and its root is rebellion towards God.

This transformational process occurs in our lives during our quiet times as we meditate upon God's truths and as we seek to allow Christ to live through us. It is vital, if you are to be transformed, that you not only hear these truths but personally know the One whose character displayed their attributes.

Rebellion is in the heart of our old nature and it is the opposite of being a servant. *Joshua 24:19-24 (NIV) [19] Joshua said to the people, "You are not able to serve the LORD. He is a holy God; he is a jealous God. He will not forgive **your rebellion and your sins**. [20] If you forsake the LORD and serve foreign gods, he will turn and bring disaster on you and make an end of you, after he has been good to you." [21] But the people said to Joshua, "No! We will serve the LORD." [22] Then Joshua said, "You are witnesses against yourselves that you have chosen to serve the LORD." "Yes, we are witnesses," they replied. [23] "Now then," said Joshua, "throw away the foreign gods that are among you and yield your hearts to the LORD,* *the God of Israel." ²⁴ And the people said to Joshua,* **"We will serve the LORD our God and obey him."**

We must understand this rebellious side of our old nature and ask Christ to enable us to crucify our selfishness and become His servants. In Thessalonians, Paul speaks about their faith saying, *I Thessalonians 1:8-10 (NIV) ⁸* **The Lord's message rang out from you** *not only in Macedonia and Achaia—<u>your faith in God has become known everywhere</u>. Therefore we do not need to say anything about it, ⁹ for they themselves report what kind of reception you gave us. They tell how you turned to God from idols* **to serve the living and true God,** *¹⁰ and to wait for his Son from heaven, whom he raised from the dead—Jesus, who rescues us from the coming wrath.*

The message of their lives rang out and the essence of their lives had changed. They no longer were serving themselves and going the ways of the world. They had become servants of the living and true God. The transformation in their lives became known everywhere. The Bible tells us they worked, endured, and turned away from the pleasures of the world. Has the transformation from being selfish to serving the living God become known about you?

We live in a very hedonistic society where our wants and desires drive us to do what we want. We are very concerned with our comforts and our entertainment. This generation has a humanistic philosophy that teaches us that we have "good" inside us and through education we can bring this good out. This type of education focuses upon what we want rather than upon what God wants. We ask questions like, "What do you want to be when you grow up?" **The appropriate question should be, "What is God's will for your life?" This should be your only focus. It should not be a self-reflection of** *what do I want or what do I like.*

When we become servants of God we surrender our wants to please our Master. We no longer are the lord of our lives, but we call on Jesus as our Lord. The Bible tells us that in governing ourselves we are to have the same attitude as that of Christ Jesus who made himself nothing, taking on the nature of a servant. What does it mean that God made himself nothing? Jesus explained what it means in *Mark 10:45 (NIV)* [45] *For even the Son of Man did not come to be served, but to serve, and to give his life as a ransom for many."*

Becoming a Servant of God is an honorable position and you will be listed among the great people of faith if you will surrender to Jesus as your Lord.

- Servant Abraham - Gen. 26:24;
- Servant Moses - Num 12:7;
- Servant Joshua - Josh. 24:29;
- Servant David - 2 Sam 7:5;
- Servant Isaiah - Isaiah 20:3;
- Servant Paul – Rom 1:1;

- Servant James – James 1:1;
- Servant Peter – 2 Pet. 1:1;
- Servant Jude – Jude 1:1

Jesus calls everyone to this role of Servant. *Mark 9:35 (NIV) ^{35} Sitting down, Jesus called the Twelve and said, "If anyone wants to be first, he must be the very last, and the servant of all."*

We must move away from the educational philosophy of our self-centered world where God's principle of being a servant has been lost. We must get back to having the right attitude in life. *Philippians 2:5-7 (NIV) ^{5} **Your attitude** should be the same as that of Christ Jesus: ^{6} Who, being in very nature God, did not consider equality with God something to be grasped, ^{7} **but made himself nothing, taking the very nature of a servant**, being made in human likeness.*

One of the main purposes of the church should be on discipleship and teaching the people to have a servant's attitude like Jesus.

In the church at Thessalonica the believers were being persecuted for their faith and they were seeking God and asking Him for the strength to endure. They were so concerned about Paul and Silas being killed for their faith that they made them leave town. They were not thinking about themselves, they were concerned servants of God putting the needs of others above their own wants and desires.

They could have said, "This is uncomfortable and hard. Paul will just have to fend for himself. I'm going to go to the church down the street that does not have such trouble." Becoming a servant of God does not mean that everything is going to be easy. The issue is more in your attitude and the position God has called you to. He has called you to be the very last and the servant of all.

CHARACTERISTICS OF A CHRIST-LIKE SERVANT

1. HUMBLE

Matthew 11:28-30 (NIV) [28] "Come to me, all you who are weary and burdened, and I will give you rest. [29] Take my yoke upon you and learn from me, for I am gentle and humble in heart, and you will find rest for your souls. [30] For my yoke is easy and my burden is light."

Jesus said, *"Come to me, all who are weary and burdened, and I will give you rest."* What makes us weary and burdened? How do we get this way? We get weary and burdened when we try to be the lord of our own lives and the lives of people around us. We get easily frustrated when people do not do what we want. We get burdened trying to please ourselves and others. Did you know that it is impossible to fulfill yourself with worldly pleasures? We were not created to be filled by our lusts and passions we are created to be filled by God. Our lusts and passions are from our corrupted nature and they can never be satisfied.

*Proverbs 27:20 (NIV) [20] Death and Destruction are **never satisfied**, and neither are the eyes of man.*

*Ecclesiastes 5:10 (NIV) [10] Whoever loves money never has money enough; whoever loves wealth is **never satisfied** with his income. This too is meaningless.*

*Ecclesiastes 6:7 (NIV) [7] All man's efforts are for his mouth, yet his appetite is **never satisfied**.*

Notice what Jesus said would give us rest, "*Take my yoke upon you and learn from me.*" A yoke is a heavy harness that fits over the shoulders of an animal. It is attached by ropes to a piece of equipment that the animals are to pull. The animals are then guided in what direction to go by their master. Does this sound like something that would give us rest? Putting a heavy yoke on our necks and being guided by another is going to give us rest?

This is exactly what will give us rest! We need to submit to the Lordship of Jesus in our lives and become His servants. By serving Him and others we will receive rest and peace.

Our weariness and burdens come from our pride. If we are successful, our pride is inflated and we try for more. If we fail at something, the rejection of others and our self-condemnation burden us with guilt and self-doubt. When we take on the yoke of Christ's attitude to serve others and build them up, we are no longer concerned about our interests and pride. This is freedom in Christ!

Jesus said, *"for I am gentle and humble in heart."* A lowly servant is concerned about meeting the needs of those around him. He is not concerned with the perception of who likes him and who does not. His character is to be gentle, meek, and humble. Humility is to be dependent upon God and to be concerned about serving others.

Through our relationship with Christ, in prayer and His Word, we learn His character and we are transformed into His likeness. Whether it is being a servant, encouraging, forgiving, humble, gentle, bold, loving God, or loving others we are transformed in our quiet times.

Paul tells us in *Philippians 2:3 (NIV) ³ Do nothing out of selfish ambition or vain conceit, but in humility consider others better than yourselves.*

Selfish ambition or vain conceit is to want praise, fame, and recognition for who we are and what we have done. It is the desire to be recognized when we enter a room. It is the feeling of being better than those around you. It is an attitude that you should be acknowledged for everything you do.

Paul tells us in *Romans 12:3-5 (NIV) ³ For by the grace given me I say to every one of you: Do not think of* *yourself more highly than you ought, but rather think of yourself with sober judgment, in accordance with the measure of faith God has given you. ^{4} Just as each of us has one body with many members, and these members do not all have the same function, ^{5} so in Christ we who are many form one body, and each member belongs to all the others.*

In the Church the only one who is to be lifted up is Jesus. Is it OK to recognize the service of others and to thank them for their hard work? Yes! But it is not OK for us to desire others to recognize us. Jesus said it this way in *Luke 17:10 (NIV) ^{10} So you also, when you have done everything you were told to do, should say, 'We are unworthy servants; we have only done our duty.'"* If we do anything good it is because Christ in us has done it. If we did not have a new nature we would still be living in our corrupted nature. It is Christ in us who is doing the good through us and we are just doing what we are told to do. Therefore, we should not seek credit for it, but we should give God all the glory for whatever good we do.

Look at this passage in *I Corinthians 4:7 (NIV) ^{7} For who makes you different from anyone else? What do you have that you did not receive? And if you did receive it, why do you boast as though you did not?*
In our corrupted state, we are selfish and prideful. We think more highly of ourselves than we ought. Which of us has created themselves? Which of us has chosen our height, looks, abilities, or blessed us with gifts? Only God has done these things. We are His

creations. Sometimes we walk around with our heads held high thinking that we are something when we are nothing. Remember our verse in Life Truth # 2, *Romans 7:18 (NIV) ¹⁸ I know that nothing good lives in me, that is, in my sinful nature.*

Humility is learning that we are completely dependent upon God to sustain us and learning to put others ahead of ourselves.

We have a corrupted flesh that desires to be served. In our corrupted flesh, we do things longing to be praised by man, or even our own children, not focusing upon being a servant and following the teachings and example of Jesus. Paul said in *Galatians 1:10 (NIV) ¹⁰ Am I now trying to win the approval of men, or of God? Or am I trying to please men? If I were still trying to please men, I would not be a servant of Christ.* Are we doing things, hoping that people will notice us and praise us? Are our motives that God would be glorified and people would be blessed according to their needs? My interests and opinions are not important, but how I serve God and others is very important. My position in this life is not to be recognized by man but to be a servant of Christ. If I am trying to please others for their approval, I am not a servant of Christ.

Are we raising the selfish or are we raising servants of God?

2. DOES NOT QUARREL OR ARGUE

A Christ-like servant is gentle, humble, and meek. This is the opposite of a prideful person. A prideful person feels like they have to argue to prove their point or be the one to win the argument. A servant just speaks on behalf of the master and does not need to defend the master. The master can defend himself.

2 Timothy 2:23-25 (NIV) [23] Don't have anything to do with foolish and stupid arguments, because you know they produce quarrels. [24] And **the Lord's servant must not quarrel**; *instead, he must be kind to everyone, able to teach, not resentful. [25] Those who oppose him he must gently instruct, in the hope that God will grant them repentance leading them to a knowledge of the truth,*
*1 Timothy 2:2 (NIV) [2] ...***that we may live peaceful and quiet lives in all godliness and holiness**.

Jesus gave us the example of living a quiet servant's life. In *1 Peter 2:23 (NIV) [23] When they hurled their insults at him, he did not retaliate; when he suffered, he made no threats. Instead, he entrusted himself to him who judges justly.*

As God's servants we are to be meeting needs and sharing the truth. If people disagree with us, we are not to be arguing, but we are to entrust ourselves to Jesus. Could your life be considered a "quiet" life? A life of quarreling, strife, and arguments is a sign that you are not being a servant of Christ. It is a sign that you are still living for your own interests and desires and you have not submitted to the yoke of Christ's leading.

*James 4:1-3 (NIV) ¹ What causes **fights and quarrels** among you? Don't they come from **your desires** that battle within you? ² **You want something but don't get it**. You kill and covet, but you cannot have what you want. **You quarrel and fight**. You do not have, because you do not ask God. ³ When you ask, you do not receive, because **you ask with wrong motives, that you may spend what you get on your pleasures**.*

Our motives should be that others would be blessed. Quarrels and fights are rooted in selfishness and pride. We must deny ourselves and learn to be the servants of all.

3. PUTS OTHERS INTERESTS AHEAD OF THEIR OWN

We are to be denying ourselves of what we want and desiring and learning to live to please God and others. Look at what *Philippians 2:3-4 (NIV) ³ Do nothing out of selfish ambition or vain conceit, but in humility consider others better than yourselves. ⁴ Each of you should look not only to your own interests, but also to the interests of others.*

Our society promotes self-centeredness. Look at the music, movies, and commercials on TV. The focus is always on your needs and wants. There is no reflection as to what God would desire. As His creations, we need to be concerned about what our creator desires.

We need to be asking God about the things we desire to see if they line up with His plan for our lives in His Word. Would God want me to have this? Would I be able to use this for God's glory? Is this something that could become an idol in my life and pull me away from God?

Paul is writing to the Philippian church when he writes about Timothy in *Philippians 2:20-21 (NIV)* [20], *I have no one else like him, who takes a genuine interest in your welfare.* [21] *For everyone looks out for his own interests, not those of Jesus Christ.*

Timothy was deeply concerned about the Spiritual maturity of the church at Philippi. His desire was for them to have an attitude like Christ Jesus being a humble servant. He took a genuine interest in their welfare, not in their happiness, but in their welfare. Would Timothy want anyone is this church to have something that would steal their affections away from Christ? Of course not! To put others interests ahead of our own is not implying that we just give people everything they want or desire. Our end purpose is to do like Paul said in *Colossians 1:28-29 (NIV)* [28] , *We proclaim him, admonishing and teaching everyone with all wisdom,* **so that we may present everyone perfect in Christ.** [29] *To this end I labor, struggling with all his energy, which so powerfully works in me.*

If an alcoholic desired a drink, we would not be acting like Christ if we gave him one. So what would it look like to put his interests ahead of our own? If we sacrificed our interests of comfort and satisfaction and we stayed with the alcoholic until that desire for a drink passed, that would be Christ-like. If we brought someone into our home to help and it disrupted our comforts for a while, that would be Christ-like. Are we serving people like this? Do we have a genuine interest in them becoming perfect in Christ?

This kind of self-sacrifice needs to be exampled and taught even in the little things. Remember it is an attitude and it is not just something we do every once in a while. It is a mental position set on being like Christ in all we do. Here are a few examples of how Jesus met needs:

- Meeting the needs of people (Water into wine John 2:1 / Loaves and fish - Matt. 14:15)
- Comfort those is trouble (Calming the storm - Matt 8:22)
- Help others out financially when you can (Paying Peter's tax - Matt. 17:24)
- Look out for those being mistreated and speak up for them (Good Samaritan - Luke 10:33)
- Come alongside the outcast (Samaritan Woman at the Well - John 4)

If you had saved the last piece of your favorite pie and you longed to eat that piece before you went to bed, what would you do if someone asked you for it? What would Jesus do if someone asked him for that last piece of pie? We know exactly what Jesus would do and we must do likewise in our new nature. In fact, we need to be looking for people to give the pie to and not just waiting for someone to ask. Who around you is in need? Who could use some encouragement? Who could use a meal or a hug or just a shoulder to cry on? Who is caught in a sin that you could help them out of?

A servant who is fulfilling his master's wishes and God's wishes is found in *Galatians 5:13-14 (NIV) ¹³ You, my brothers, were called to be free. But do not use your freedom to indulge the sinful nature; rather, serve one another in love. ¹⁴ The entire law is summed up in a single command: "Love your neighbor as yourself."* We must learn to put our wants and interests aside and serve others for their benefit.

4. LOOKS TO JESUS FOR THEIR EXAMPLE

Matthew 20:25-28 (NIV) ²⁵ Jesus called them together and said, "You know that the rulers of the Gentiles lord it over them, and their high officials exercise authority over them. ²⁶ Not so with you. Instead, whoever wants to become great among you must be your servant, ²⁷ and whoever wants to be first must be your slave– ²⁸ just as the Son of Man did not come to be served, but to serve, and to give his life as a ransom for many."

God's will for your life is that you put your wants and interests at the bottom of your list and you live to serve God and others. When need to raise a generation of servants of Christ. As we look at the future generation, do we see selfless, hardworking servants or do we see individuals only concerned about their wants and desires? If we see the latter, we need to remember that the apple does not fall far from the tree. Have we raised a generation of servants? Are we an example what a Christ-like servant is like?

Jesus' greatest example of how a servant needs to be is when he gave up his life for us on the cross. Isaiah (Chapter 53) refers to him as the suffering servant. His needs took second place to the needs of others. He died for our benefit. He didn't need to. He didn't have to. He was concerned about our fate, He died for us. Jesus not only died for us, but for everyone, even those who will never accept Him.

He revealed to his disciples in John (Chapter 13) the full extent of his love when he washed their feet. Their dirty smelly feet. The Lord himself knelt down as their servant and he washed them. He did not do it with a begrudging heart or a bad attitude, but with a genuine concern for their needs. He even washed Judas' feet with a gentle, humble, loving spirit.

Is your life an example of such a genuine concern for the needs and interests of others? Would you wash people's feet because you are concerned about them or would you just care about your own needs and wonder who is going to wash your feet? Would you wash the feet of your enemies? If you are seeking to be like Christ and to be His servant, then go and do likewise. Your focus must be to please God and to love others like He does.

Don't forget that at some point Jesus looked down and noticed that your feet were dirty. He not only noticed, but he decided to do something about it. *John 13:4 (NIV) [4] so he got up from the meal, took off his outer clothing, and wrapped a towel around his waist.* His outer clothing was his royal robes. He wrapped the humble towel of human flesh around him. After he had humbled himself by dying on the cross for you, he gently came and knelt before you and politely asked if he could wash your dirty feet. He knelt with a specific purpose. His purpose was to clean the dirt off you with the water in the basin, his purifying blood. The dirt did not affect him at all, but he could see that the dirt was affecting you greatly. It was causing you to behave in ways that were harming you. He knew that if the dirt was not removed, it would eventually kill you and send you to hell. When Jesus knelt before Peter he said, *"[8] "No, you shall never wash my feet." Jesus answered, "Unless I wash you, you have no part with me." John 13:8 (NIV)* Unless Jesus washes your feet we will have no part with him.

When he had finished washing the disciples' feet he asked them in, John 13:12-17 (NIV) *[12]"Do you understand what I have done for you?" [13] "You call me 'Teacher' and 'Lord,' and rightly so, for that is what I am. [14] Now that I, your Lord and Teacher, have washed your feet, you also should wash one another's feet. [15] I have set you an example that you should do as I have done for you. [16] I tell you the truth, no servant is greater than his master, nor is a messenger greater than the one who sent him. [17] Now that you know these things, you will be blessed if you do them.*

Will we do the same for others? Do we see the dirt on others and yet are we too selfish to help them? Will we sacrifice our time, money, and energy to minister to others? Will we be so concerned about the dirt on other peoples' feet that it will cause us to take the position of a servant and help them for their benefit?

This life truth about being created to serve is so deep that we must meditate upon it. In our sinful flesh, we have little desire to serve others. But with Christ in us, we learn to lay our lives down and meet the needs of those around us. Not in the way that they think we should meet them, but in the godly way that they need. We must be an example and raise up servants of Christ who do not argue when things are not going their way. We cannot be lazy and self-centered. We must genuinely care about the needs of others, their interests, and the progress of their faith.

WORKSHEET FOR SELF-GOVERNMENT
LIFE TRUTH # 4
I AM CREATED TO SERVE

Question: Does our old nature want to serve others?
Answer: No, it does not. We must crucify our old nature and learn to serve.

> *Mark 10:43-44 (NIV) ^{43} (Not so with you. Instead), whoever wants to become great among you must be your servant, ^{44} and whoever wants to be first must be slave of all.*
>
> Write out the Life Truth, question, and answer on one side of an index card and the verse on the other side. Keep it in your Bible for the week. Work on it every day individually and as a family. Have it memorized by next week.

Read Matthew 24:45-51 and answer the following questions.
What could symbolize "a faithful servant giving someone their food at the proper time"?

The wicked servant was assigned a place in hell for his disobedience. What was his disobedience?

Could we beat others with our words? How?
Read Luke 10:25-37 and answer the following questions.

The Samaritan, whom the Jews were prejudice against, was considered the neighbor because of his actions towards the one in need. What is this parable trying to tell us about our prejudices towards others?

What did it take for the Samaritan to help this man?

What was the Samaritans view about "his" money?

Almost every day we cross paths with people. Are we looking for those that we can serve? If not, why not? How can we be more aware and ready to serve others?

A servant has put their interests and desires to the side to serve others. Quarreling and arguing is a sign that you are seeking to get your desires met. Read these verses 1 Thess. 4:11; 1 Tim 2:2; James 4:1-3; and answer the following questions. Why do we fight and quarrel?

Instead of quarreling what should our focus be?

How can focusing on meeting the needs of others help our fights and arguments?

What are the some of the differences between a selfish person and a servant of Christ?

Based on this LIFE TRUTH what area(s) do you need to be working on to continue crucifying your old nature? Could your life be considered a quiet life or a quarrelling life?

SELF-GOVERNMENT
LIFE TRUTH # 5
I AM CREATED TO PRAISE

Human praise of God is a central theme in Scripture. The word praise is listed over 330 times in the Bible. It comes from the Latin word meaning to "value". Therefore, when we praise God, we are proclaiming His greatness and His goodness. The book of Psalms means "Praises", and comes from the same Hebrew root word as "hallelujah" which means "Praise the Lord."

We learned in the last life truth that we are to be the servants of God. The Scriptures declare that the servants are to praise the Lord. *Psalm 113:1-3 (NIV) [1] Praise the LORD. Praise,* **O servants of the LORD, praise the name of the LORD.** *[2] Let the name of the LORD be praised, both now and forevermore. [3] From the rising of the sun to the place where it sets, the name of the LORD is to be praised.* The New Testament reveals that the name of the Lord is Jesus, so we are to Praise Jesus! This truth is declared over and over in the Scriptures and is one of the main reasons each one of us has been created. The name of the Lord is to be praised and God's creations are created to declare praise to God!

No one is excluded from praising God. *Isaiah 43:21 (NIV) [21] the people I formed for myself* **that they may proclaim my praise.**

*Psalm 150:6 (NIV) ⁶ **Let everything** that has breath praise the LORD.*

Jesus told us that the greatest purpose for our lives is in *Matthew 22:37-38 (NIV) ³⁷ ... "'Love the Lord your God with all your heart and with all your soul and with all your mind.' ³⁸ This is the first and greatest commandment.*

When we love God with all of our being this causes us to worship, praise, rejoice, be thankful, and glorify. Each of these attributes has a different meaning but they are all closely related.

Worship is to acknowledge the presence of God. Praise is a response of worship. Thankfulness is a part of praise and a response to blessings given. To glorify is to bestow honor, praise, and admiration. Rejoicing is to have great delight and give praise.

*Matthew 4:10, Jesus says, "Worship the Lord your God and serve him only." - Psalm 29:2 says, "Give unto the Lord **the glory due his name**; worship the Lord in the beauty of holiness."*

We are not only to be praising God but we are to be rejoicing in Him every day! Many times we think praise is just something we do as a congregation on Sunday, but God commands it to be a daily part of our lives.

*Philippians 4:4 (NIV) ⁴ Rejoice in the Lord **always**. I will say it again: Rejoice!*

*1 Chronicles 16:8-10 (NIV) ⁸ **Give thanks** to the LORD, **call on his name**; **make known** among the nations what he has done. ⁹ **Sing** to him, sing praise to him; **tell of all his wonderful acts**. ¹⁰ **Glory** in his holy name; let the hearts of those who seek the LORD **rejoice.***

When we think about worship and praise, we may only think about singing. But it is so much more. It is shouting, declaring, telling, bowing, clapping, making God known, being prostrate, praying, living a holy life, and more. It is about who you are and what you love. If you are passionate about Jesus and what he has done for you, then you will worship and praise Him!

Praise is tied into the first two of the Ten Commandments where God says that we should have no others gods before Him and we are not to have any idols. This keeps us focused on giving God the praise due his name and our hearts from being drawn away to love something more than Him.

WHERE DOES WORSHIP AND PRAISE COME FROM?

a. It comes from our new nature

As we learned in our second Self-Government life truth there is no one who seeks God. Within our corrupt nature we do not want to praise God. The Scriptures declare in, *1 Corinthians 12:3 (NIV) ³ Therefore I tell you that no one who is speaking by the Spirit of God says, "Jesus be cursed," and no one can say,*

"Jesus is Lord," except by the Holy Spirit. Christ in us is what enables us to fulfill our responsibility to praise the Lord. Without the Holy Spirit in us, we will not praise the Lord. The phrase "Jesus be" or "Jesus is" is more about the character changes within us and not just saying the specific phrase. Do we acknowledge God for our blessings? Or do we think that somehow we have deserved them? Or that we deserve better than we have?

b. It comes from a heart fully committed to God.

We are to crucify what we want to do and be fully committed to Christ. This is the process of praise! As we surrender everything to God, we realize that His design for every one of us is to praise Him! *I Kings 8:61 (NIV) ⁶¹ But your hearts must be fully committed to the LORD our God, to live by his decrees and obey his commands, as at this time." 2 Chronicles 16:9 (NIV) ⁹ For the eyes of the LORD range throughout the earth to strengthen those whose hearts are fully committed to him. I Peter 3:15 (NIV) ¹⁵ But in your hearts set apart Christ as Lord.*

We must remember that we are corrupt. We desire to be the center of attention. We desire for worship and praise to be directed towards us. All of us deal with this self-centered attitude. Some have the *"look at me"* attitude for what I have done; and some have the *"woe is me"* attitude for not being praised enough

for what I have done. This self-focus attitude needs to die and Christ alone needs to be praised!
We are told that to be a servant of God we must make ourselves the slaves of all. If we are seeking to receive the praises of men, we are not servants of Christ. Christ's servants are to be the instruments of God's praise. It is our corrupt flesh that fights against this new nature. Our hearts must be fully committed to God. But whose heart can do that? Not one of us can by ourselves. That's why we must humble ourselves and ask for God's assistance in this matter. Only Christ in us can fulfill such a request! We praise when we become passionate about God. Praise is deeper than just singing songs to God. It is the attitude of gratefulness and gratitude towards God. It flows from new hearts of humbleness, thankfulness, and awe directed towards the awesome God who created us, loved us, and gave himself for us.

SOME CHARACTERISTICS OF PRAISE

Humility - *I Chronicles 29:20 (NIV) [20] Then David said to the whole assembly, "Praise the LORD your God." So they all praised the LORD, the God of their fathers; they bowed low and fell prostrate before the LORD and the king.*

Dancing - *Psalm 149:3 (NIV) [3] Let them praise his name with dancing and make music to him with tambourine and harp.*

Singing - *Psalm 135:3 (NIV) ³ Praise the LORD, for the LORD is good; sing praise to his name, for that is pleasant. Psalm 147:1 (NIV) ¹ Praise the LORD. How good it is to sing praises to our God, how pleasant and fitting to praise him! Psalm 149:1 (NIV) ¹ Praise the LORD. Sing to the LORD a new song, his praise in the assembly of the saints.*

We are commanded to sing praises to God individually and together as congregations. This is why churches have services which include congregational singing. Some people are gifted singers. Some people have the ability to lead others in worship. Sometimes we sing out loud and at other times we sing in our hearts to the Lord.

Lifting up hands - *Psalm 63:4 (NIV) ⁴ I will praise you as long as I live, and in your name I will lift up my hands.*

Standing - *Nehemiah 9:5-6 (NIV) ⁵...: "Stand up and praise the LORD your God, who is from everlasting to everlasting." "Blessed be your glorious name, and may it be exalted above all blessing and praise.*

Living a righteous life - *Romans 12:1-2 states, "Therefore, I urge you, brothers, in view of God's mercy, to offer your bodies as living sacrifices, holy and pleasing to God – **this is your spiritual act of worship.** Do not conform any longer to the pattern of this world, but be transformed by the renewing of your mind. Then you will be able to test and approve what God's will is – his good, pleasing and perfect will." –*

Love for one another - *Romans 15:7 (NIV) ⁷ Accept one another, then, just as Christ accepted you, **in order to bring praise to God.***

Abstaining from Immorality - *1 Peter 2:11-12 (NIV) ¹¹ Dear friends, I urge you, as aliens and strangers in the world, to abstain from sinful desires, which war against your soul. ¹² Live such good lives among the pagans that, though they accuse you of doing wrong, **they may see your good deeds and glorify God** on the day he visits us.*

Good deeds - *Matthew 5:16 (NIV) ¹⁶ In the same way, let your light shine before men, that they may see your good deeds and **praise your Father in heaven.***

As Christians, we are to be the light illuminating Jesus. Picture a dark room with several people struggling to find their way. Then picture someone turning on a flashlight. After your eyes focus on the object in the light you see Jesus. This is to be our lives. The things we do and say should point people to Jesus. Our sacrificial serving of others should not only point people to Jesus but also bring Him praise. This is the meaning of *1 Corinthians 10:31 (NIV) ³¹ So whether you eat or drink or whatever you do, **do it all for the glory of God.***

Colossians 3:17 (NIV) ¹⁷ And whatever you do, whether in word or deed, do it all in the name of the Lord Jesus, giving thanks to God the Father through him. Everything that we do is to bring praise and glory to God. What does your flashlight illuminate?

HOW CAN WE MAKE SURE THAT OUR PRAISE (OR LIGHT) ILLUMINATES JESUS?

1. UNDERSTAND THAT PRAISE IS POWERFUL

*Psalm 29:2 (NIV) ² **Ascribe** to the LORD the glory due his name; worship the LORD in the splendor of his holiness.* Ascribe means to give credit where credit is due. God is the creator and sustainer of all and therefore is He is due all praise. When we praise God, it pleases Him, and He begins to move on our behalf.

*Psalm 67:5-6 (NIV)⁵ May the peoples praise you, O God; may all the peoples praise you. ⁶ **Then** the land will yield its harvest, **and God, our God, will bless us**.* The Bible declares that the land yielded a harvest because the people praised God. Notice what this passage says about the rebellious in *Psalm 68:6 (NIV) ⁶ God sets the lonely in families, he leads forth the prisoners with singing;* ***but the rebellious live in a sun-scorched land.***

God's provisions and blessings are released and sustained when we praise him. We are told in *Deuteronomy 8:10 (NIV) ¹⁰ When you have eaten and are satisfied, **praise the LORD** your God for the good land he has given you.* If we do not, we become arrogant and proud, and we begin to believe that we have somehow deserved the blessings of God.

When was the last time that you thanked God for his many blessings in your life? Do you thank him daily? Do you praise him for your blessings? Notice what this self-government passage tells us about God's will for our lives. *1 Thessalonians 5:16-18 (NIV) [16] Be joyful always; [17] pray continually; [18] give thanks in all circumstances, for this is God's will for you in Christ Jesus.*

We are to be joyful, prayerful, and thankful always! I AM CREATED TO PRAISE.

2. ADMIT THAT GRUMBLING AND COMPLAINING IS SIN

A.W. Tozer said, "Without worship, we go about miserable." How would people define you? Do you have a downcast spirit that grumbles and complains or one that is joyful, and thankful?

The opposite of praise is grumbling and complaining. Do you remember the Israelites whom God delivered out of Egypt? As He was leading them to the Promised Land, they grumbled against God. At first, they grumbled about the food so God gave them quail and manna. Then they grumbled about the land, flowing with milk and honey, being inhabited. They were to eat from plants they did not plant. But they could only see the BIG people. They did not remember how BIG GOD was and that He could remove them. They forgot the miraculous power of God in the plagues and what the Lord did to Pharaoh's army. Eventually, God had enough.

*Numbers 14:26-33 (NIV) [26] The LORD said to Moses and Aaron: [27] "How long will this wicked community grumble against me? I have heard the complaints of these grumbling Israelites. [28] So tell them, 'As surely as I live, declares the LORD, I will do to you the very things I heard you say: [29] In this desert your bodies will fall—every one of you twenty years old or more who was counted in the census **and who has grumbled against me.** [30] Not one of you will enter the land I swore with uplifted hand to make your home, except Caleb son of Jephunneh and Joshua son of Nun. [31] As for your children that you said would be taken as plunder, I will bring them in to enjoy the land you have rejected. [32] But you—your bodies will fall in this desert. [33] Your children will be shepherds here for forty years, **suffering for your unfaithfulness**, until the last of your bodies lies in the desert.*

Not only did the grumbling generation not enter into the Promised Land but their children suffered for it. Complaining and grumbling is a sin and it does not reflect a people who have been redeemed from the grave by God.

*Philippians 2:14-15 (NIV) [14] Do **everything** without complaining or arguing, [15] so that you may become blameless and pure, children of God without fault in a crooked and depraved generation, in which you shine like stars in the universe.*

If you are complaining you are sinning! If you are complaining you are not praising. This life truth is not I AM CREATED TO COMPLAIN! We are not only to praise God ourselves, but we are to teach our children to praise God. (Psalm 78)

3. REALIZE THAT PRAISING GOD CAUSES US TO BE FILLED WITH THE SPIRIT

The Scriptures tell us that we have a responsibility to be filled with the Spirit in *Ephesians 5:18-20 (NIV)* [18] *Do not get drunk on wine, which leads to debauchery. Instead, be filled with the Spirit.* Then in verse 19 Paul reveals to us how we are filled with the Spirit. [19] *Speak to one another with psalms, hymns and spiritual songs. Sing and make music in your heart to the Lord,* [20] **always giving thanks** *to God the Father for everything, in the name of our Lord Jesus Christ.* When God's people praise He enthrones himself in their midst. *Psalm 22:3 (NIV)* [3] *Yet you are the Holy One enthroned on the praises of Israel.*

When we praise Him, He takes delight in us, and He moves on our behalf. *Psalm 149:2-6 (NIV)* [2] *Let Israel rejoice in their Maker; let the people of Zion be glad in their King.* [3] *Let them praise his name with dancing and make music to him with tambourine and harp.* [4] **For the LORD takes delight in his people**; *he crowns the humble with salvation.* [5] *Let the saints rejoice in this honor and sing for joy on their beds.* [6] *May the praise of God be in their mouths and a double-edged sword in their hand.*

This is some of the power that we can experience through praise:

a. It pulls us out of depression

Psalm 42:5 (NIV) ⁵ Why are you downcast, O my soul? Why so disturbed within me? Put your hope in God, for I will yet praise him, my Savior and my God. The Psalmist repeats this same verse in Psalm 42:11, and 43:5. We need to keep telling our downcast souls to praise, even forcing them to praise at times. The Holy Spirit longs for us to give praise to Jesus. We must crucify our old flesh and let our praises ring out! Sing, declare, tell of His works, shout, and dance before the Lord our God!

b. It begins a healing in our afflictions

Psalm 69:29-31 (NIV) ²⁹ I am in pain and distress; may your salvation, O God, protect me. ³⁰ I will praise God's name in song and glorify him with thanksgiving. ³¹ This will please the LORD more than an ox, more than a bull with its horns and hoofs. Psalm 34:1-3 (NIV) ¹ I will extol the LORD at all times; his praise will always be on my lips. ² My soul will boast in the LORD; let the afflicted hear and rejoice. ³ Glorify the LORD with me; let us exalt his name together.

c. It empowers us in our trials

Acts 16:22-26 (NIV) ²² The crowd joined in the attack against Paul and Silas, and the magistrates ordered them to be stripped and beaten. ²³ After they had been severely flogged, they were thrown into prison, and the jailer was commanded to guard them carefully. ²⁴ Upon receiving such orders, he put them in the inner cell and fastened their feet in the stocks. ²⁵ **About midnight Paul and Silas were praying and singing hymns to God**, *and the other prisoners were listening to them. ²⁶ Suddenly there was such a violent earthquake that the foundations of the prison were shaken.* **At once all the prison doors flew open, and everybody's chains came loose.**

d. It gives us endurance in our persecutions
Matthew 5:11-12 (NIV)¹¹ "Blessed are you when people insult you, persecute you and falsely say all kinds of evil against you because of me. ¹² **Rejoice and be glad**, *because great is your reward in heaven, for in the same way they persecuted the prophets who were before you.*

e. It brings the presence of God
2 Chronicles 5:13-14 (NIV) ¹³ The trumpeters and singers joined in unison, as with one voice, to give praise and thanks to the LORD. Accompanied by trumpets, cymbals and other instruments, **they raised their voices in praise to the LORD and sang: "He is good; his love endures forever."** <u>Then</u> *the temple of the LORD was filled with a cloud, ¹⁴ and the priests could not perform their service because of the cloud, for the glory of the LORD filled the temple of God.* Today we are the temple of the Holy Spirit and the awesome presence of the almighty God fills us when we praise Him.

PRAISE IS NOT OPTIONAL

As we talked about the evidence of salvation earlier, we must understand that praise is not optional in a believer's life. One of the evidences that we have been born again is that we declare the praises of God. Serious reflection needs to be taken in the life of a believer who does not praise. If you do not praise the Lord, there is a good possibility that you do not have a new nature.

Evidence of your salvation is that you praise the Lord. *I Peter 2:9 says, "But you are a chosen people, a royal priesthood, a holy nation, a people belonging to God, **that you may declare the praises of him** who called you out of darkness into his wonderful light."*

If the only thing God did for us was to send His son Jesus to die on the cross for our sins, saving us from an eternal hell, then that alone would be enough to praise Him for all eternity. But God did so much more than that! He gave us life twice. He created us and then He redeemed us from the grave. He never treats us as our sins deserve. God gives us new mercies every day. He purifies us from all unrighteousness and crowns us with love and compassion. He is close to the broken-hearted and is a father to the fatherless. He heals all our diseases and defeated death for us. He frees us from the power of sin. He anoints our heads with oil and He restores our souls. He has given us His Holy Spirit and has made us co-heirs with Christ!

You might say where do I start? I know I am not praising God enough! Don't feel alone. All of us can grow in this area. Confess your ungratefulness to the God, who took your sin upon himself to free you from an eternal hell, and declare His praises!

It is in our obedience that we see God move. Obedience equals blessings. We must obey God's command to praise, to experience His blessings in our lives. Remember the story of Jericho in *Joshua 6:2-5 (NIV)* *² Then the LORD said to Joshua, "See, I have delivered Jericho into your hands, along with its king and its fighting men. ³ March around the city once with all the armed men. Do this for six days. ⁴ Have seven priests carry trumpets of rams' horns in front of the ark. On the seventh day, march around the city seven times, with the priests blowing the trumpets. ⁵ When you hear them sound a long blast on the trumpets, have all the people give a loud shout; then the wall of the city will collapse and the people will go up, every man straight in."*

God gave the command to the people and they had to obey. What if the people decided not to march around the city? What if they decided we are only going to go around three times and that will be enough? What if they shouted every time they went around? The walls would have remained! It is by obeying God's Word that we see results.

The people obeyed the Lord and look what happened in *Joshua 6:20 (NIV)* *²⁰ When the trumpets sounded, the people shouted, and at the sound of the trumpet,* **when the people gave a loud shout, the wall collapsed;** *so every man charged straight in, and they took the city.*

When they had obeyed God, just as He prescribed, the wall collapsed. Are you struggling with depression, an affliction? Are you going through a trial, a persecution? Or do you just desire the presence of God more in your life? Then obey God and realize that you are created to praise!

Psalm 30:10-12 (NIV) [10] Hear, O LORD, and be merciful to me; O LORD, be my help." [11] You turned my wailing into dancing; you removed my sackcloth and clothed me with joy, [12] that my heart may sing to you and not be silent. O LORD my God, I will give you thanks forever.

Psalm 86:12-13 (NIV) [12] **I will** *praise you, O Lord my God, with all my heart;* **I will** *glorify your name forever. [13] For great is your love toward me; you have delivered me from the depths of the grave.*

WORKSHEET FOR SELF-GOVERNMENT
LIFE TRUTH # 5
I AM CREATED TO PRAISE

Question: Does our old nature want to praise the Lord?
Answer: No, it does not. We must crucify our old nature and praise the Lord.

> Colossians 3:16 (NIV) [16] Let the word of Christ dwell in you richly as you teach and admonish one another with all wisdom, and as you sing psalms, hymns and spiritual songs with gratitude in your hearts to God.
>
> Write out the Life Truth, question, and answer on one side of an index card and the verse on the other side. Keep it in your Bible for the week. Work on it every day individually and as a family. Have it memorized by next week.

The Bible considers the righteous saved and the wicked condemned. From these verses what is different about their character? (Psalm 32:11; 64:10; Psalm 107:42-43)
The Righteous R_____ and P_____ .
The Wicked S_____ their mouths.

We are commanded in the Scriptures not to steal and if anyone does steal they are sinning against God.

In the same way, we are commanded to praise, so if a person refuses to praise what are they doing?

What are the consequences of sin? (Hint: Deut. 28:15)

Read Psalm 68:3-4. Does this verse describe you? If not, reflect on why not and write down what you need to change to obey God in this area.

Read Psalm 42:5; 97:12 Should my praise be dependent upon my feelings?

What should we do if we do not feel like praising? Read 2 Chronicles 20:1-30. What did the Israelites do when faced with a problem? (verse 3,4)

According to verse 13 who was at their meeting?

In verse 21 Jehoshaphat appointed men to do what?

What happened when they began to sing? (verse 22)

In verse 27 it says that, "the Lord had given them cause to rejoice." Did they praise before or after the victory? A. Before B. After C. Both Why is this truth important?

The Valley of Beracah means what? Valley of _____. What are some practical things that you can do to help you praise God more?

Based on this LIFE TRUTH what area(s) do you need to be working on to continue crucifying your old nature and praising God more?

The Righteous Praise and the Wicked shut their mouths. (Psalm 32:11; 64:10; Psalm 107:42,43)

SELF-GOVERNMENT
LIFE TRUTH # 6
I AM CREATED TO ENCOURAGE

The Bible tells us in *1 Thessalonians 5:11 (NIV)* *11 "Therefore **encourage one another** and **build each other up**, just as in fact you are doing."* As we continue to learn about our new nature in Christ, the need to crucify self to fulfill God's purpose for our lives becomes much clearer. We are created in this new nature to serve, to praise, and also to encourage.

To encourage means to inspire with hope, courage, and to spur on.

Biblical **hope** is more than a "worldly" hope where we simply long for our dreams to come true. Biblical hope is founded in what God has done and in the certainty that God will fulfill His promises in the future. Christians place their hope in Christ alone and His promise to someday bring them into heaven. Paul said in *Acts 23:6 (NIV)* *6 I stand on trial because of **my hope in the resurrection of the dead.**"* This kind of hope is encouraging to us and gives us confidence and boldness knowing that one day God will either call us home to be with Him or Christ will return for us. In 2 Corinthians Paul is speaking about the Spirit of God being in us and he says in *2 Corinthians 3:12 (NIV)* *12 Therefore, since we have **such a hope, we are very bold.***

Courage is mental and moral strength to endure; to be very bold and confident. Courage is sometimes translated as *confidence* in Scripture. In *Hebrews 3:6 (NIV) ⁶ But Christ is faithful as a son over God's house. And we are his house, if we hold on to our **courage** and the hope of which we boast.* The same Greek Word is in *Hebrews 4:16 (NIV) ¹⁶ Let us then approach the throne of grace with **confidence (or courage),** so that we may receive mercy and find grace to help us in our time of need.*

To **spur** means to stimulate strongly. The book of Hebrews speaks about spurring one another in *Hebrews 10:24 (NIV) ²⁴ And let us consider how we may **spur** one another on toward love and good deeds.* The word "spur" gives us a visual picture of a rider spurring his horse to get it going. We are to strongly stimulate each other toward love and good deeds according to God' Word.

Biblical encouragement is more than just saying kind words to one another. We are to be continually instilling courage in others to accomplish one specific goal. The goal is to be like Christ. Our task is to encourage people as they grow stronger and mature in Christ. I Thessalonians 5:11 says that we are to lay our lives down to "*encourage and build each other up.*" It is our mission to see that everyone succeeds in their relationship with Christ.

As we mature in our praise to God, we must also grow in our encouragement of others. Both of these areas are rooted in Scripture. We encourage one another by speaking the very words of God. Our flesh finds faults with others, but our Spirit encourages them.

We are not only told in the Scriptures to encourage one another, but we are told in *Hebrews 3:13 (NIV)* [13] *But **encourage one another daily**, as long as it is called Today, so that none of you may be hardened by sin's deceitfulness.* We need to focus on filling each other with courage, hope, and confidence daily; faithfully keeping our eyes on Jesus and His return!

WHERE DO WE GET OUR ENCOURAGEMENT FROM?

1. From God

We get our courage directly from God. In *2 Thessalonians 2:16-17 (NIV)* [16] *May our Lord Jesus Christ himself and God our Father, who loved us and by his grace gave us **eternal encouragement** and **good hope**,* [17] ***encourage your hearts and strengthen you*** *in every good deed and word.*

Psalm 10:17 (NIV) [17] *You hear, O LORD, the desire of the afflicted;* ***you encourage them****, and you listen to their cry,*

When the apostle Paul was in prison, the Jews, in Jerusalem, stirred up a riot to try and have him killed. But during the night, Paul encountered a visitor who encouraged him. It says in *Acts 23:11 (NIV)* *[11] The following night **the Lord** stood near Paul and said, **"Take courage!** As you have testified about me in Jerusalem, so you must also testify in Rome."* When we are walking with God and following his ways, we get our encouragement directly from the Lord!

2. From God's Word

God's Word is what increases our faith and inspires courage within us. Studying the Old Testament gives us confidence in the future. Knowing about God's deliverance and miraculous powers from stories throughout the Bible, gives us confidence that He will also raise us from the dead. In *Romans 15:4 (NIV)* *[4] <u>For everything that was written in the past was written to teach us</u>, so that **through endurance** and the **encouragement of the Scriptures** we might have **hope.***

The Word is to dwell in us richly. It is through His Word that we have the encouragement to live unashamedly for Christ in this generation. *Deuteronomy 31:8 (NIV)* *[8] The LORD himself goes before you and will be with you; he will never leave you nor forsake you. Do not be afraid; do not be discouraged."* This promise is repeated in the New Testament in *Hebrews 13:5 (NIV)* *[5] ..."Never will I leave you; never will I forsake you."*

When we stop meditating on the Word daily, we begin to lose our courage and we forget about obeying the Lord. Deuteronomy 4:9 (NIV) **⁹ Only be careful, and watch yourselves closely so that you do not forget the things your eyes have seen or let them slip from your heart as long as you live. Teach them to your children and to their children after them.**

In Deuteronomy 6:20-25 (NIV) ²⁰ it says, In the future, when your son asks you, "What is the meaning of the stipulations, decrees and laws the LORD our God has commanded you?" ²¹ tell him: "We were slaves of Pharaoh in Egypt, but the LORD brought us out of Egypt with a mighty hand. ²² Before our eyes the LORD sent miraculous signs and wonders—great and terrible—upon Egypt and Pharaoh and his whole household. ²³ But he brought us out from there to bring us in and give us the land that he promised on oath to our forefathers. **²⁴ The LORD commanded us to obey all these decrees and to fear the LORD our God, so that we might always prosper and be kept alive, as is the case today. ²⁵ And if we are careful to obey all this law before the LORD our God, as he has commanded us that will be our righteousness."**

We need to be retelling the stories of what God has done for us, so that future generations will know how to serve Him. We must encourage everyone to remain true to God and His Word, in order that it might go well with us. This generation is experiencing the consequences of our disobedience. We must encourage all Christians to turn back to God now!

3. From others

We are told to encourage others. Many examples of encouragement are found in Scripture. In Acts 20:1-2 (NIV) *¹ When the uproar had ended, Paul sent for the disciples and, after **encouraging** them, said good-by and set out for Macedonia. ² He traveled through that area, **speaking many words of encouragement to the people**, and finally arrived in Greece,*

Preachers are to be instruments of encouragement. In 1 Corinthians 14:3 (NIV) *³ But everyone who prophesies speaks to men for their strengthening, **encouragement** and comfort.*

When we hear that others are walking in righteousness, it is encouraging to us. It says in 2 Corinthians 7:13 (NIV) *¹³ By all this we are **encouraged**. In addition to **our own encouragement**, we were especially delighted to see how happy Titus was, because **his spirit has been refreshed by all of you**.*

Paul illustrated this several times. He sent others back to the churches to encourage them by sharing with them his faithfulness and telling them what God was doing. Tychicus was sent to the church in Ephesus and Colosse.

*Ephesians 6:21-22 (NIV) ²¹ **Tychicus**, the dear brother and faithful servant in the Lord, will tell you everything, **so that you also may know how I am and what I am doing**. ²² I am sending him to you for this very* *purpose, that you may know how we are, and that he may encourage you.*

Colossians 4:7-8 (NIV) [7] **Tychicus** *will tell you all the news about me. He is a dear brother, a faithful minister and fellow servant in the Lord.* [8] **I am sending him to you for the express purpose that you may know** *about our circumstances and that he may encourage your hearts.*

Timothy was sent to Thessalonica in *I Thessalonians 3:1-4 (NIV)* [1] *So when we could stand it no longer, we thought it best to be left by ourselves in Athens.* [2] **We sent Timothy,** *who is our brother and God's fellow worker in spreading the gospel of Christ,* **to strengthen and encourage you in your faith,**

TELL PEOPLE THAT YOU LOVE THEM AND THAT YOU BELIEVE IN THEM -

BIBLICAL ENCOURAGEMENT HAS A PURPOSE

The purpose is as Paul stated in *Colossians 1:28-29 (NIV)* ⋯*that we may present* **everyone** *perfect in Christ.* [29] *To this end I labor, struggling with all his energy, which so powerfully works in me.* This is our life's goal: We are to make disciples, faithfully committing ourselves to them so that they may become perfected in Christ. We are to lay down our lives to serve everyone. We must encourage our families, our friends, and even our enemies. Our goal should be that everyone becomes perfected in Christ!

Here are some Biblical examples of encouragement:

- **Encourage others to be loving** - *Philemon 1:7 (NIV) [7] Your love has given me great joy and encouragement, because you, brother, have refreshed the hearts of the saints.*

- **Encourage the timid** - *1 Thessalonians 5:14 (NIV) [14] And we urge you, brothers, warn those who are idle, **encourage the timid**, help the weak, be patient with everyone.*

- **Encourage the young men to be self-controlled** - *Titus 2:6 (NIV) [6] Similarly, encourage the young men to be self-controlled.*

- **Encourage others to repent** - *2 Corinthians 7:13 (NIV) [13] By all this (speaking of their repentance) we are encouraged. In addition to our own **encouragement**, we were especially delighted to see how happy Titus was, because his spirit has been refreshed by all of you.*

- **Encourage others to keep meeting together** - *Hebrews 10:24-25 (NIV) [24] And let us consider how we may spur one another on toward* *love and good deeds. ²⁵* **Let us not give up meeting together, as some are in the habit of doing, but let us encourage one another–** *and all the more as you see the Day approaching.*

- **Encourage others not to have an unbelieving heart** - Hebrews 3:12-13 (NIV) *¹² See to it, brothers, that **none of you has a sinful, unbelieving heart** that turns away from the living God. ¹³ **But encourage one another daily,** as long as it is called Today, so that none of you may be hardened by sin's deceitfulness.*

- **Encourage others with sound doctrine -** Titus 1:9 (NIV) *⁹ He must hold firmly to the trustworthy message as it has been taught, so that he can **encourage others by sound doctrine** and refute those who oppose it.*

KEYS TO BIBLICAL ENCOURAGEMENT

1. Keep a Kingdom focus

Moses, after he had displayed anger, was not allowed to lead the people into the Promised Land. In our spiritual journey, it is never about us! It is always about God getting the glory for the things that we do. Moses took credit for the water coming out of the rock when he struck the rock in anger and said in Numbers 20:10 (NIV) *¹⁰ "Listen, you rebels, **must we bring you water** out of this rock?"* This is the sin that

110

kept Moses from leading the people into the Promised Land. Moses could have become negative and bitter. After all, he had led the people through the plagues, through the Red Sea, and then through 40 years of wandering in the desert because of their grumbling. Moses blamed the people when he told them about God's new plan, but he also submitted himself to God and His will. He focused the rest of his life on encouraging another man to lead. This encouraging of the next generation is vital! If we are to return to God in our nation, we must invest our lives in the lives of others by encouraging and strengthening young men and women to become a new generation of godly leaders. We must encourage the nation to be Christian again.

God told Moses to commission Joshua to lead the people. *Deuteronomy 3:28 (NIV)* [28] *But commission Joshua, and* **encourage and strengthen him,** *for he will lead this people across and will cause them to inherit the land that you will see."*

In the New Testament, Jesus has become our leader and we are commanded to follow Him - *Matthew 16:24 (NIV)* [24] *Then Jesus said to his disciples, "If* **anyone** *would come after me, he must deny himself and take up his cross* **and follow me.**

Our goal, as Christians, is to follow Jesus so closely that we can say to others like Paul said in *1 Corinthians 11:1 (NIV)* [1] *Follow my example, as I follow the example of Christ.* If we are not there, yet, we can still encourage them to keep a Kingdom focus by saying *Ephesians 5:1 (NIV)* *[1] Be imitators of God, therefore, as dearly loved children.* Or *I John 2:6 (NIV) [6] Whoever claims to live in him must walk as Jesus did.* This is our goal in encouragement that we would present everyone perfect in Christ!

Biblical encouragement is so much more than just saying nice things to people; like *"you look nice today."* It should keep spiritual matters at the forefront of your mind. Salvation is the greatest miracle in life. Without salvation, a person will spend an eternity in Hell. So our goal is not just to tell people when they look nice, but to encourage them to come to know Christ and to mature in Him. When Paul is speaking to the Church at Corinth he begins to tell them his credentials for being a minister. It says in *2 Corinthians 3:1-4 (NIV) [1] Are we beginning to commend ourselves again? Or do we need, like some people, letters of recommendation to you or from you? [2]* ***You yourselves are our letter****, written on our hearts,* ***known and read by everybody****. [3] You show that you are a letter from Christ, the result of our ministry, written not with ink but with the Spirit of the living God, not on tablets of stone but on tablets of human hearts. [4] Such confidence as this is ours through Christ before God.*

Paul's confidence for being a minister was that people were being born again and looking like Christ. This is our goal in encouragement! Our desire should be to see people born again and brought into the Kingdom of God. Paul takes no credit for what God is doing in his life when he says in 2 *Corinthians 3:5,6* *⁵ Not that we are competent in ourselves to claim anything for ourselves, but our competence comes from God. ⁶* **He has made us competent as ministers of a new covenant***–not of the letter but of the Spirit; for the letter kills, but the Spirit gives life.*

This is evidence that Paul is saved and that he is fulfilling his purpose of encouraging people. Later in the letter, Paul says that we are all to be ministers: 2 *Corinthians 5:17-19 (NIV) ¹⁷ Therefore, if anyone is in Christ, he is a new creation; the old has gone, the new has come! ¹⁸ All this is from God, who reconciled us to himself through Christ* **and gave us the ministry of reconciliation:** *¹⁹ that God was reconciling the world to himself in Christ, not counting men's sins against them.* **And he has committed to us the message of reconciliation.**

What good does it really do for others if all we say are things like: *You look nice. You did a great job. You have a nice house.* These things are not wrong, and they should be said, but they definitely do not go deep enough. We must encourage others with Biblical encouragement: encouraging young men to be self-controlled; encouraging the timid; encouraging people not to have unbelieving hearts; encouraging people not to give up meeting together; encouraging sinners to repent; and encouraging everyone at all times with sound doctrine. It is of no benefit to people if we tell them they look nice and they end up in hell. Looking nice in hell will count for nothing!

2. Look for the weak in heart

Have you noticed that being a Christian here on this earth can be hard? We are not to love the things of this world. We are not to participate in pagan things or chase after our own lusts. We are to forgive and love our enemies. We are to give thanks in all circumstances. We are to witness, serve, praise, and encourage. We will look like aliens and strangers to the world when we follow Christ. We will even get persecuted for it. The writer of Hebrews writes to the church to encourage them not to lose heart and to stay focused on the promise of heaven! Do you know anyone going through a hard time? Do you know anyone who is discouraged? Then, walk alongside them and encourage them. Remind them of this passage in *Hebrews 12:1-11 (NIV)* *¹ Therefore, since we are surrounded by such a great cloud of witnesses, let us throw off everything that hinders and the sin that so easily entangles, and let us run with perseverance the race marked out for us. ² <u>Let us fix our eyes on Jesus, the author and perfecter of our faith, who for the joy set before him endured the cross</u>, scorning its shame, and sat down at the right hand of the throne of God. ³ <u>Consider him who endured such opposition from sinful men</u>,* **so that you will not grow weary and lose heart. ⁴ In your struggle against sin, you have not yet resisted to the point of shedding your blood.** *⁵ And you have forgotten that* **word of encouragement** *that* *addresses you as sons:* **"My son, do not make light of the Lord's discipline, and do not lose heart when he rebukes you,** [6] *because the Lord disciplines those he loves, and he punishes everyone he accepts as a son."* [7] *Endure* **hardship** *as discipline; God is treating you as sons. For what son is not disciplined by his father?* [8] *If you are not disciplined (and everyone undergoes discipline), then you are illegitimate children and not true sons.* [9] *Moreover, we have all had human fathers who disciplined us and we respected them for it. How much more should we submit to the Father of our spirits and live!* [10] *Our fathers disciplined us for a little while as they thought best; but God disciplines us for our good, that we may share in his holiness.* [11] **No discipline seems pleasant at the time, but painful.** *Later on, however, it produces a harvest of righteousness and peace for those who have been trained by it.*

Remind them that Jesus endured the cross for us and at times he allows us to go through hard things because He loves us. His desire for us is holiness. If we go through His discipline with thankfulness and praise, we will become stronger, having more courage and confidence than we did before. Help them to praise God in all circumstances and redirect their complaining hearts. Place new courage within them through Biblical encouragement. Have them memorize Psalm 23 with you and declare it together! *Psalm 23:4-6 (NIV)* [4] *Even though I walk through the valley of the shadow of death, I will fear no evil, for you are with me; your rod and your staff, they comfort me.* [5] *You prepare a table before me in the presence of my enemies. You anoint my head with oil; my cup overflows. ⁶ Surely goodness and love will follow me all the days of my life, and I will dwell in the house of the LORD forever.*

We are a powerful witness when we give thanks and praises to God through our trials. It shows the world that we know our future home is being prepared for us in heaven. This life is only temporary as Jesus told us John 16:33 (NIV) *³³ "I have told you these things, so that in me you may have peace. In this world you will have trouble. But take heart! I have overcome the world."* Who could you share an encouraging verse with? Who do you know that is weak in heart and could use a hug and some spiritual nourishment?

3. Supply what is lacking

All of us are corrupt individuals and have areas we can work on to become more Christ-like. As believers, we are to be supporting one another in love and working toward the goal of maturing in Christ. In our old nature, we become fault finders; but in our new nature, we become encouragers. It is easy for us to see what is lacking in other people, but it takes the work of the Holy Spirit for us to *supply* what is lacking in others. Look at *I Corinthians 16:17 (NIV) ¹⁷ I was glad when Stephanas, Fortunatus and Achaicus arrived,* **because they have supplied what was lacking from you.**

Jude 1:16 talks about evil men who were faultfinders. These men could easily point out the faults of others.

It was obvious to them what people were lacking, being blinded about their own sin of pride. We can easily follow our old nature and get into this fault-finding mode. But when we do, we look more like the devil, who is called the accuser in Revelations 12:10. Remember, the opposite of encourager is faultfinder.

Look at what Paul did when he saw something lacking in another's faith in *1 Thessalonians 3:10 (NIV)* *[10] **Night and day we pray most earnestly** that we may see you again **and supply what is lacking in your faith.*** Paul supplied what was lacking in their faith. He spoke the truth in love and prayed earnestly that Christ would perfect them in their short-coming. Our corrupt nature accuses, gossips, complains, and finds fault in others. But our new nature, prays earnestly and walks alongside others to supply what is lacking. We could transform our families, churches, and communities if we would encourage others like this! Is there something lacking in your spouse or in another relationship? Are you faultfinding or are you earnestly praying and supplying what is lacking? A complaining accuser will not encourage another to be more like Christ. Their words will bring discouragement, strife, and tear the other person down. This faultfinding attitude brings disgrace to the name of Christ. As one of God's children, you did not learn to accuse from Him. You are not following Him if you point out the faults of others. *James 1:5 (NIV)* *[5] If any of you lacks wisdom, he should ask God,* *who gives generously to all without finding fault, and it will be given to him.*

A recent news story, which aired on a CBS show called "On the Road Again," credited a young man who made a decision to place the success of another his priority. The student who succeeded in the story had a disability and had been the team manager of a high school basketball team. In his last game as manager, the coach decided to suit him up and play him in the game. The manager's name was Mitchell Marcus. When Mitchell entered the game, in the final minutes, his team did everything they could to help him score a basket. But in spite of their efforts, and Mitchell taking a few shots, there was still no success. Their final attempt to get Mitchell to succeed in making a basket, resulted in Mitchell missing the pass, and the ball going out of bounds to other team. What happened next is an awesome illustration of encouraging another. A senior player on the other team held the ball to pass it in for the final play of the game. But instead of passing the ball to his team, he decided to, as he put it, "Treat others as he would want to be treated." He called out Mitchell's name, who happened to still be standing by his basket, and he threw him the ball. Mitchell turned around, shot the ball, and made the basket just as the buzzer sounded! Here is the link to the news story: http://www.cbsnews.com/8301-18563_162-57570865/act-of-sportsmanship-gives-texas-high-schooler-shot-at-glory/

We all have disabilities. We all have areas that we can improve upon. As the body of Christ, we are all in this perfecting business together. *Galatians 6:1-2 (NIV) ¹ Brothers, if someone is caught in a sin, you who are spiritual should restore him gently. But watch yourself, or you also may be tempted. ² Carry each other's burdens, and in this way you will fulfill the law of Christ.*
We fulfill the law of Christ when it is our goal that others succeed in their faith. Can you help carry their burden and encourage them to succeed?

4. Look for the righteousness in them

Many times Paul had to encourage Christians through some very tough issues like pride, selfishness, idolatry, greed, prostitution, sexual immorality and adultery. Most of the time, we are not even dealing with these kinds of issues and we still would rather point out the faults of others. In *Romans 1:8-12 (NIV) ⁸ First,* **I thank my God through Jesus Christ for all of you, because your faith** *is being reported all over the world… ¹⁰* **in my prayers at all times***; and I pray that now at last by God's will the way may be opened for me to come to you. ¹¹* **I long to see you so that I may impart to you some spiritual gift to make you strong***–* ¹² *that is, that you and I may be* **mutually encouraged** *by each other's faith.*
In the letter to the Romans, Paul dealt with selfishness, homosexuality, hypocrites, and other sins, yet, he did it all in love. First, he said something that he could praise them for. *"I thank God for all of you, because of your faith."* Next he was in prayer over

them and finally he longed to see them to impart a spiritual gift to them and to fill them with courage! Can you thank God for the person that you have found fault with? Will you pray earnestly for God to impart a spiritual gift to them so that you both can be mutually encouraged? Are you so focused upon what is lacking in them that you cannot even see the righteousness that Christ is doing through their life? If someone was going to share with you an area that you were lacking in, how would you want them to tell you? You would want someone who you knew loved you and saw some good in you. You would like to hear some good news before the bad news. Transform your relationships and begin to biblically encourage others.

1. Thank them for the righteous things they are doing
2. Pray for them about what is lacking in their lives
3. Come alongside them to fill what is lacking

Last week we learned that we are to do everything without complaining. We are not to be complaining about what is lacking in people, but we are to be encouraging them toward love and good deeds. Would people say that you are an encourager or a faultfinder?

Look at Paul's example:

***1 Corinthians** 1:4 (NIV)* ⁴ *I always thank God for you because of his grace given you in Christ Jesus;*

***Philippians** 1:3-4 (NIV)* ³ *I thank my God every time I remember you.* ⁴ *In all my prayers for all of you, I always pray with joy;*

***Colossians** 1:3 (NIV)* ³ *We always thank God, the Father of our Lord Jesus Christ, when we pray for you;*

***1 Thessalonians** 1:2-3 (NIV)* ² *We always thank God for all of you, mentioning you in our prayers.* ³ *We continually remember before our God and Father your work produced by faith, your labor prompted by love, and your endurance inspired by hope in our Lord Jesus Christ.*

Do you know who Joseph the Levite was? Most people don't know him by that name because the apostles called him Barnabas. *Acts 4:36 (NIV)* ³⁶ *Joseph, a Levite from Cyprus, whom the apostles called Barnabas (which means Son of Encouragement).*

Barnabas was called *son of encouragement* by the men who walked with Jesus. What an awesome title to be given. When Saul got converted on the road to Damascus and became Paul, he ended up in Jerusalem and wanted to join the apostles. The Bible says in *Acts 9:26 (NIV)* ²⁶ *When he came to Jerusalem, he tried to join the disciples, but they were all afraid of him, not believing that he really was a disciple.* Could you imagine? Saul was the man who is going around arresting Christians, throwing them in jail, and having some of them killed for their faith. This man wanted to meet with the apostles. If you were in their shoes would you be afraid? Would you want to be arrested by this very powerful man of the Sanhedrin and the Romans? Would you be afraid of being separated from your family, possibly thrown in jail, and most likely even killed for your faith?

They may have heard what they believed to be rumors of his conversion, but they were sure this was just a trick to get them in his presence.

Would you have the courage to face him? Would you be willing to meet with this man? What man would have the courage to come face to face with such an anti-Christ individual? The *son of courage!* That's who. Barnabas. Barnabas was not afraid of Saul or any man for that matter. He was courageous! Just as God intends for all of us to be. He was a man like Joshua who heeded the words spoken by God to Joshua.

Joshua 1:6-9 (NIV) ⁶ "Be strong and courageous, because you will lead these people to inherit the land I swore to their forefathers to give them. ⁷ Be strong and very courageous. Be careful to obey all the law my servant Moses gave you; do not turn from it to the right or to the left, that you may be successful wherever you go. ⁸ Do not let this Book of the Law depart from your mouth; meditate on it day and night, so that you may be careful to do everything written in it. Then you will be prosperous and successful. ⁹ **Have I not commanded you?** *Be strong and courageous. Do not be terrified; do not be discouraged, for the LORD your God will be with you wherever you go."*

This is very similar to our call in the New Testament in *1 Corinthians 16:13 (NIV) ¹³ Be on your guard; stand firm in the faith; be men of courage; be strong.*

The Bible says in *Acts 9:27-28 (NIV) ²⁷ But* **Barnabas took him and brought him** *to the apostles.* **He told them** *how Saul on his journey had seen the Lord and that the Lord had spoken to him, and how in Damascus he had preached fearlessly in the name of Jesus. ²⁸* **So Saul stayed with them** *and moved about freely in Jerusalem, speaking boldly in the name of the Lord.*

Barnabas saw what was lacking in Saul and he came alongside him and spoke up for him. It was Barnabas who brought him to the disciples. Barnabas wasn't concerned about his own welfare or reputation. He was concerned about Saul. If Saul really had converted, then he was going to be hated by the Sanhedrin. What used to be Paul's companions would have now become his enemies and Saul needed a friend. Barnabas put his own reputation on the line. If the disciples would have been unwilling to meet with Saul, after Barnabas had befriended Saul, then there would have been a real possibility that the apostles would no longer meet with Barnabas.

In your new nature, you are made to be men and women of courage!! Your new nature is longing to impart this courage to others so they may know God and be right with Him. Knowing that someday, when He returns, they will be welcomed into the Kingdom of Heaven.

We are to be building others up, according to their needs, that it may benefit those who listen. Fault finding, accusing, and complaining words are not to be come out of our mouths. Are you imparting courage within others or are you discouraging them with your words and actions?

WORKSHEET FOR SELF-GOVERNMENT
LIFE TRUTH # 6
I AM CREATED TO ENCOURAGE

Question: Does our old nature want to encourage others?
Answer: No, it does not. We must crucify our old nature and encourage others.

> Hebrews 3:13 (NIV) ¹³ But encourage one another daily, as long as it is called Today, so that none of you may be hardened by sin's deceitfulness.
>
> Write out the Life Truth, question, and answer on one side of an index card and the verse on the other side. Keep it in your Bible for the week. Work on it every day individually and as a family. Have it memorized by next week.

According to these verses what are we to be encouraging others to do?
Titus 2:6 –

Hebrews 3:12-13- Not have a S_____
U_____ H_____ Hebrews 10:24, 25- Not give up M_____
T_____

What did the apostles call Joseph the Levite in Acts 4:36? B_____ Son of
_____

Read Acts 12:25 -13:5 – Who was with Barnabas and Saul on their missionary journey?

Read Acts 13:13; 15:36-38 – What did John Mark do on their missionary journey?

Read Acts 15:39-41 – Who did Barnabas take with him?_____ What did Barnabas do for John Mark that encouraged him?

Later in Paul's life he asked for this person to come and visit him _____ (2 Tim 4:11; Acts 12:25) Do you think Barnabas giving John Mark a second chance had anything to do with Paul now saying he was useful to him? Why?

What lesson of encouragement can we learn from Barnabas when people let us down? (How does this verse relate Matthew 18:21, 22)

We are told in 1 Thessalonians 5:11 to "encourage and build others up." What do these verses tell us about building others up? Ephesians 4:29; Proverbs 12:18; 16:24

The opposite of encouraging is faultfinding. We can many times see what is lacking in others, but are we willing to do what I Cor. 16:17; 1 Thess. 3:10 says? What would this look like?

Based on this LIFE TRUTH what commitments do you need to make to be a better encourager? Who can you encourage this week? (Spend time in your Life Group encouraging each member)

SELF-GOVERNMENT
LIFE TRUTH # 7
I AM CREATED TO WITNESS

The twentieth century American culture is telling us that we must keep our faith out of the public square. Our culture doesn't want the Ten Commandments in courtrooms; it doesn't want nativity scenes in public buildings or at public parks; it doesn't want praying before, during, or even after school. What should we do? Should we obey what our culture tells us or should we obey God?

Jesus told his followers to *"Go"* and share their faith in the public arena. *Matthew 28:18-20 (NIV)* [18] *Then Jesus came to them and said,* **"All authority in heaven and on earth** *has been given to me.* [19] *Therefore go and make disciples* **of all nations,** *baptizing them in the name of the Father and of the Son and of the Holy Spirit,* [20] *and* **teaching them to obey everything** *I have commanded you. And surely I am with you always, to the very end of the age."*

If the authorities tell us that we are not to bring our faith into the public square, then they are asking us to disobey God. Who is the highest authority that we should obey? Jesus answered this question when He made the statement, *"All authority in heaven and on earth has been given to me."* Jesus is the ultimate authority in heaven and on earth. He created the four institutions and told us how to govern ourselves in each institution. One institution of self-government that we must obey is being a witness for Christ to all nations.

We are to *"make disciples of all nations, and teach them to obey everything Christ commanded."* To make disciples of all nations is to take our faith and belief system into the public square. We cannot separate our faith from our everyday life. Our faith is to transcend into everything we do and say. As born-again believers, we are no longer ordinary; we are transformed into courageous, bold, witnesses of Christ.

Acts 4:13 (NIV) **¹³ When they saw the courage** of *Peter and John and realized that* **they were unschooled, ordinary men**, <u>they were astonished</u> **and they took note that these men had been with Jesus.** God can take the ordinary, unschooled and make them bold and courageous! So much so that it will astonish those around them.

Does our faith astonish those around us? Are we being the bold, courageous witnesses that Christ has called us to be? Are we seeing our nation become more Christian or less Christian? Are we seeing our own state, community, neighborhood, and family become more Christian?

Isaiah tells us that we are to be God's witnesses. Isaiah *43:11-12 (NIV)* ¹¹ says, I, even I, am the LORD, *and apart from me there is no savior.* ¹² *I have revealed and saved and proclaimed– I, and not some foreign god among you.* **You are my witnesses**,*" declares the LORD, "that I am God."*

To witness is to give evidence and to testify about something we know or have had personal experience with. To testify is to express a personal conviction. Our faith is a personal conviction. God wants us to witness by sharing our personal convictions about Him. We will bring glory to the name of Jesus by obeying what He has said. What would happen to our family, neighborhood, community, state, and nation if we witnessed like the early church did? What would happen to me if I believed that God could use me to change my community? What would happen in our community if we laid our agendas down and we went out to teach those around us the Word of God?

A WITNESS IS DECLARING WHAT THEY KNOW

This needs to be the first order of business before we look at what a witness does. If I am to go out and witness for Christ, I must have some first-hand experience with Him. Jesus said in *John 17:3 (NIV)* [3] **Now this is eternal life: that they may know you,** *the only true God, and Jesus Christ, whom you have sent.* If we have not had an experience with God, how can we express Him to others? If we do not know Christ Jesus, how can we tell others what He is like and what He has done for us? One of the greatest tragedies in the church today is the number of people who believe they are saved, but have no relationship with Christ. Jesus said that eternal life is that we know God, not that we know about Him, but that we personally know Him.

I grew up attending church every time the doors were open. My family and I were members of Maplewood Baptist Church near St. Louis, Missouri. I remember attending Vacation Bible School in the summer when I was in fifth grade. During one of the VBS sessions, the pastor called for those who wanted to be saved to come forward. My very best friend felt God's call to be saved and headed down the aisle. I, on the other hand, being very curious about what was going on, followed behind. I repeated the prayer that the minister told me to say and was baptized a few weeks later. Everyone seemed to be proud of the decision I had made. I even felt pretty good about it myself.

The only problem was, I wasn't saved. I was not born again. I did not repent of my sins and make Jesus my Lord. There was no indwelling of the Holy Spirit. This same tragedy that happened to me, happens to people in churches everywhere. Many people believe that they are saved, but they do not have a new nature. The scary thing is that these people are on their way to hell unless they hear the truth.

Too often, we have believed the lie that "good" people go to heaven, especially the "good" people who pray a prayer. This is not the teachings of Christ. The Bible says that when Jesus began to preach he preached repentance. *Matthew 4:17 (NIV) *¹⁷* **From that time on** Jesus began to preach, "**Repent**, for the kingdom of heaven is near."* Repentance is to stop living the way you think is right and make Jesus the Lord of your life and follow Him. We must follow Jesus by obeying the Bible and doing what it commands us to do.

When I was seventeen, I had a genuine experience with salvation. I was born again! How do I know? What was different? I was not even at church. I was in my bedroom when I cried out to God saying, *"Lord, if you're real, I will serve you the rest of my life."* At that point, something happened to me that I will never forget. The Spirit of Almighty God entered me and gave me a new nature. Prior to praying that prayer, I was under heavy conviction, filled with guilt and shame for some things that I had done. After the prayer, I felt cleansed, renewed, and forgiven. I felt so good that I even began to giggle.

 I know that my testimony will not be exactly like the testimony of another, but there are two things that every testimony should have in common. The first is repentance and the second is being born again. You may not giggle like I did; you may not pray exactly what I prayed; you may not be alone in your room; but the one thing you will know for sure is that Christ is in you. The fact is that to be Biblically saved you must repent and call Jesus your Lord! If you do not repent, and make Jesus your Lord, you will not be saved.

When you **know**, that you **know**, that you **know,** you will witness for Jesus because of the amazing thing that He has done for you. One of the immediate changes in my nature was my love for God's Word. Before being born again, the Word was just another book. Afterwards, it was like fuel for the new fire that burned within me. Do you have a hunger, at all, for God's Word? Do you have a longing to obey Him and bring Him glory? Do you have a desire to serve, praise, encourage, and witness? If not, perhaps, you are like I was in the fifth grade, a baptized person who prayed, but not a person who had a new nature.

Look at what Paul says in 2 Corinthians 13:5 (NIV) 5 Examine yourselves to see whether you are in the faith; test yourselves. Do you not realize that Christ Jesus is in you--unless, of course, you fail the test? God enables us to repent and respond to the gospel.

Romans 10:9-10 (NIV) ⁹ That if you confess with your mouth, "Jesus is Lord," and believe in your heart that God raised him from the dead, you will be saved. ¹⁰ For it is with your heart that you believe and are justified, and it is with your mouth that you confess and are saved.

Confess Jesus as your Lord and obey what Christ said in *Luke 9:23-24 (NIV) ²³ Then he said to them all: "If anyone would come after me, he must deny himself and take up his cross daily and follow me.* ²⁴ *For whoever wants to save his life will lose it, but whoever loses his life for me will save it.*

IN CHRIST, THE UNSCHOOLED AND ORDINARY BECOME BOLD AND COURAGEOUS

1. God has chosen you

Do you ever feel like you might be the last one picked if people had to choose teams? Perhaps, that's happened to you recently, or when you were younger. Who would choose me? Who would want me on their team?

Jesus desires that everyone be on His team. Every single person that has been created has been created by the hands of Christ with special care and made in the image of God. *Colossians 1:16 (NIV) ¹⁶ For by him **all things** were created: things in heaven and on earth, visible and invisible, whether thrones or powers or rulers or authorities; **all things** were created by him and for him.* Our sin separated us from God and if God was a man he would have given up on us, but God is not like us. Even though we sinned against Him, he still desires for us to be on His team. The Bible says in, *I Timothy 2:3-4 (NIV) God our Savior, ⁴ **who wants all men to be saved** and to come to a knowledge of the truth.* He so badly wants us on His team that He died for everyone's sin on the cross. *2 Corinthians 5:15 (NIV) ¹⁵ And he died for all.* Everyone who accepts His

134

invitation and calls upon Him as Lord can be on His team.

*Mark 13:27 (NIV) ²⁷ And he will send his angels and gather **his elect** from the four winds, from the ends of the earth to the ends of the heavens. I Thessalonians 1:4 (NIV) ⁴ For we know, brothers loved by God, **that he has chosen you,***

*I Corinthians 1:26-29 (NIV) ²⁶ Brothers, think of what you were **when you were called**. Not many of you were wise by human standards; not many were influential; not many were of noble birth. ²⁷ **But God chose** the foolish things of the world to shame the wise; **God chose** the weak things of the world to shame the strong. ²⁸ **He chose** the lowly things of this world and the despised things—and the things that are—to nullify the things that are, ²⁹ so that no one may boast before him.*
No matter how we feel about ourselves, God picked us to be a part of His family.

We must receive the invitation to be under His leadership and accept the call to follow Him. Being chosen means that we have responsibilities to fulfill. It says in *John 15:16 (NIV) ¹⁶ **You did not choose me, but I chose you**, and appointed you to go and bear fruit—fruit that will last.*

2. God has equipped you
How can I have the courage to speak up? Who would listen to me? Why would anybody think that I have something to say?

I love the passage in Acts that talks about the unschooled and ordinary astonishing others.

Acts 4:13 (NIV) [13] **When they saw the courage** of Peter and John and realized that **they were unschooled, ordinary men,** <u>they were astonished</u> and **they took note that these men had been with Jesus.**

Wow! What a testimony that these men had. Guess what? This is to be our lives. We are to be witnessing as the apostles did. Did you know that even Paul was afraid to witness? *I Corinthians 2:1-5 (NIV)* [1] *When I came to you, brothers, I did not come with eloquence or superior wisdom as I proclaimed to you the testimony about God.* [2] *For I resolved to know nothing while I was with you except Jesus Christ and him crucified.* [3] **I came to you in weakness and fear, and with much trembling.** This is the same feeling that many of us get when we think about witnessing. But Paul goes on to say, [4] *My message and my preaching were not with wise and persuasive words,* **but with a demonstration of the Spirit's power,** [5] *so that your faith might not rest on men's wisdom, but on God's power.*

When we begin to speak boldly for Jesus and His word, God gives us the courage and strength to declare His message.

I have been struggling with witnessing ever since I was saved. It has gotten easier, but there are still times when I would just rather remain silent. I am ashamed to admit that I have had witnessing opportunities where I remained silent instead of speaking up. Thankfully, God is a forgiving God who loves us and forgives us when we confess our sins. It's time for our generation to rise up in the power of the Holy Spirit and speak boldly just like the church of Acts did.

a. With the Holy Spirit

In the fourth chapter of Acts, the early church was being persecuted because the culture was telling them to remain silent about Jesus. They were not only told to be silent, but they were being arrested, killed, and separated from their families. In our generation, the persecution has not risen to that level, but we still need to speak up and disciple others. The church came together for encouragement. They cried out to God for help and for the ability to speak with boldness. Look at what happened after they prayed, *Acts 4:31 (NIV) [31] After they prayed, the place where they were meeting was shaken. And they were all filled with the Holy Spirit and spoke the word of God boldly.*

I am not against passing out tracts or inviting people to church. But if that is all we do, we are not fulfilling the commission of teaching them everything. The early church was empowered by the Holy Spirit to speak the Word of God boldly. We need the same empowering today!

When we are born again, we receive the Holy Spirit. *Ephesians 1:13 (NIV) [13] And you also were included in Christ when you heard the word of truth, the gospel of your salvation. Having believed, you were marked in him with a seal, the promised Holy Spirit,* Look at what Jesus said in *Acts 1:8 (NIV) [8] But* **you will receive power when the Holy Spirit comes on you; and you will be my witnesses** *in Jerusalem, and in all Judea and Samaria, and to the ends of the earth."*

b. With His Word

Many Christians say to themselves, *"What would I say if I witnessed?"* There are others who witness, but are sharing an incomplete gospel. The command of Christ to *"go and make disciples"* is tied to the fact that we are to be *"teaching them to obey everything that Christ commanded."* We are not to just hand out tracts and get people to pray a prayer. We are to be teaching people to obey the Scriptures.

It is time for us to be people of the Word. People, who know the Word, live by the Word, and who proclaim the Word to others. 2 Timothy 3:15 tells us that the Holy Scriptures are able to make us wise for salvation through faith in Christ Jesus.

Be intentional and understand the power of God's Word. We already learned that the Scriptures are able to make us wise for salvation. It says in *Hebrews 4:12 (NIV) [12] For the word of God is living and active. Sharper than any double-edged sword, it penetrates even to dividing soul and spirit, joints and marrow; it judges the thoughts and attitudes of the heart.* When we share the Word with others, it will begin to do a work in them. We are also told in *1 Peter 4:11 (NIV) ¹¹ If anyone speaks, he should do it as one speaking the very words of God.* You cannot get any closer to speaking the very words of God than when you are sharing verses with people. Share specific passages from the Bible with others. Teach them what the Word of God says. Show them the four institutions in Scripture and their responsibilities. Show them the Life Truths. Teach them to obey everything.

We need to stop wondering about what to say, and start sharing the Word of God with others today. Share the Life Truths with others. Take your Bibles everywhere you go. Be ready to share all that Christ has taught you in His Word.

The life truths are a great starting point for making disciples. Not only can you learn the truths yourself, but you can share them with the people around you. Every week you have a new verse to share with your neighbors, co-workers, friends, and family. You can ask them questions like, *"Did you know that all Scripture is inspired by God?"* When they say, *"No,"* or that they don't believe that, you can either quote them the verse in 2 Timothy 3:16,17 or you can show them the verse from your Bible.

Did you know that God's Word says that...
- All Scripture is God breathed – 2 Tim. 3:16

- There is no one who seeks God – Rom. 7:18
- We have a corrupted nature that needs to be crucified – Gal. 2:20
- In God's Kingdom we are to be the greatest servants – Mark 10:43,44
- We are created to praise God – Col. 3:16
- We are created to encourage others – Heb. 3:13
- We are created to witness – Rom. 1:16

In Matthew 5:14 Jesus told us to go out and be the light of the world. What does light do? It expels the darkness and drives it back. When we are sharing the Word, we are driving back the darkness.

Look at this passage in, *Matthew 4:12-17 (NIV) [12] When Jesus heard that John had been put in prison, he returned to Galilee. [13] Leaving Nazareth, he went and lived in Capernaum, which was by the lake in the area of Zebulun and Naphtali– [14] to fulfill what was said through the prophet Isaiah: [15] "Land of Zebulun and land of Naphtali, the way to the sea, along the Jordan, Galilee of the Gentiles– [16] the people living in darkness have seen a great light; on those living in the land of the shadow of death a light has dawned." [17] From that time on Jesus began to preach, "Repent, for the kingdom of heaven is near."*

Jesus is called the Light and He is also called the Word. When we witness by sharing the Word of God with others, we expel the darkness! By speaking God's Word to others, we are speaking the very words of God. Plant God's Word in people's hearts because the *"Holy Scriptures are able to make us wise for Salvation."* Trust God's Word to do its work!

3. God has sent you

One of the greatest obstacles that we have with witnessing is our focus. When our focus is off, we will not hit the target we are aiming for. You cannot point a gun in the opposite direction of the target and expect to hit it. Our target is to "make disciples".

Many have said, *"I could never do that"* and they have turned their backs on the target. Here's a little incentive for you to try. Jesus said in, *Luke 9:26 (NIV) [26] If anyone is ashamed of me and my words, the Son of Man will be ashamed of him when he comes in his glory and in the glory of the Father and of the holy angels.* Being a witness of God's Word is not optional for Christians. Christians witness and non-believers remain silent.

Our focus must be on the commission that God has given us to make disciples. Jesus said in *Luke 19:10 (NIV) [10] For the Son of Man came to seek and to save what was lost."* He also said in *Matthew 4:19 (NIV) [19] "Come, follow me, and I will make you fishers of men."*

Compare what Christ said to what Paul said in *I Corinthians 10:33 (NIV) [33] even as I try to please everybody in every way. For I am not seeking my own* *good but the good of many, **so that they may be saved.** Romans 10:1 (NIV)* ¹ *Brothers, **my heart's desire and prayer** to God for the Israelites **is that they may be saved.** I Corinthians 9:22 (NIV)* ²² *To the weak I became weak, to win the weak. I have become all things to all men **so that by all possible means I might save some.***

This is the essence of the verse in *Galatians 2:20 (NIV)* ²⁰ *I have been crucified with Christ and I no longer live, but Christ lives in me.* The Holy Spirit was living Christ's life through Paul. Because of Paul's surrendered life, he saw God do amazing things.

Notice again the passage in *John 15:16 (NIV)* ¹⁶ *You did not choose me, but I chose you and appointed you to go and bear fruit–fruit that will last.* **Then the Father will give you whatever you ask in my name.** The Bible tells us to go out and bear fruit. This means to make disciples by teaching them to obey His Word. God, in turn, promises to do amazing things for us when we obey His commands. The Father will give you whatever you ask in Christ's name. Do you want to see your loved one saved? Do you want to see the bars and other immoral establishments in your town closed? Do you desire to see prayer and the Bible back in our public school systems?

The asking must be focused upon the right target. If we fix our eyes on Jesus, and we are seeking to do his will, God will do the impossible through us. In Matthew 14, Jesus takes a roll of bread and some fish, feeding over 5000 people. He does the impossible. After this miracle, the Bible says in *Matthew 14:22-33 (NIV)* *²² Immediately Jesus made the disciples get into the boat and go on ahead of him to the other side, while he dismissed the crowd. ²³ After he had dismissed them, he went up on a mountainside by himself to pray. When evening came, he was there alone, ²⁴ but the boat was already a considerable distance from land, buffeted by the waves because the wind was against it. ²⁵ During the fourth watch of the night Jesus went out to them, walking on the lake.* Most of our pictures of Jesus walking on the water depict Him walking on a calm lake, but the Bible says that the boat was buffeted by the waves. The fourth watch is a 3am to 6am Roman time period. The disciples had been on the water all night, struggling to get to the other side, when they saw Jesus walking on the waves. His appearance terrified them. *²⁶ When the disciples saw him walking on the lake, they were terrified. "It's a ghost," they said, and cried out in fear.* Immediately Jesus spoke to them *²⁷ But Jesus immediately said to them:* **"Take courage! It is I. Don't be afraid."**

Jesus told them to "Take courage!" Just like He told Paul in Acts 23:11 when He commissioned him to witness in Rome. Peter then asked to do the impossible, *²⁸ "Lord, if it's you," Peter replied, "tell me to come to you on the water." ²⁹ "Come," he said. Then Peter got down out of the boat, walked on the water and came toward Jesus.* The Bible says we have not, because we ask not. Why did only one of the twelve ask to do the impossible? Peter does the impossible and he walks on water. Why was Peter able to walk on the water? Because he asked God for it. Ask God to do the impossible! Remember what Jesus was doing most of the night? Praying. Peter asked and the Lord responded. Ask God to bring back your wayward loved one; ask God to save the lost around you; ask God to change your family, neighborhood, community, and nation; ask God to give you the courage to be a bold witness for Him.

The Bible then says, *^{30} But when he saw the wind, he was afraid and, beginning to sink, cried out, "Lord, save me!"* When we take our eyes off of Jesus, we lose the focus of our target and we begin to sink. Stay focused on Jesus! Praise Him! Do not look at the circumstances around you. Stop thinking only about what is possible. Start asking God for the impossible! Continue to praise Him through everything!

When we get in trouble, we need to cry out to Jesus and He will save us,*^{31} Immediately Jesus reached out his hand and caught him. "You of little faith," he said, "why did you doubt?" ^{32} And when they climbed into the boat, the wind died down. ^{33} Then those who were in the boat worshiped him, saying, "Truly you are the Son of God."* If we stay focused on what Jesus has done for us and continue to worship Him for it, we will be much better witnesses. God saved them from the buffeting waves; Jesus saved us from hell. Worship him, praise His holy name, become a witness boldly declaring what Christ has done in your life. Be a joyful witness, rejoicing in the Lord always!

Tell your heart to remind your face that you are saved, so that your witness will be powerful and believable. Stay in the Word daily in order to keep your fire burning. *Psalm 19:7-9 (NIV) ⁷ The law of the LORD is perfect, **reviving the soul.** The statutes of the LORD are trustworthy, **making wise the simple.** ⁸ The precepts of the LORD are right, **giving joy to the heart.** The commands of the LORD are radiant, **giving light to the eyes**.* The Word revives us. It makes the unschooled and ordinary wise. It brings joy to our hearts, and gives light to the eyes of everyone who reads it.

God has not saved me from the buffeting waves, but he has saved me from hell and the punishment of my sins! It is time to tell the world how Jesus has changed your life!

Church, it is our responsibility to keep building courage within each other, staying focused on our mission to make disciples. We are to be teaching each other and speaking to one another with psalms, hymns, and spiritual songs. We are to remain thankful and grateful for what the Lord has done for us and what He will do in the future. When Christ's purpose becomes ours, we will see God do amazing things. NOW GO AND MAKE DISCIPLES!

WORKSHEET FOR SELF-GOVERNMENT
LIFE TRUTH # 7
I AM CREATED TO WITNESS

Question: Does our old nature want to witness to others?
Answer: No, it does not. We must crucify our old nature and learn to witness.

> Philemon 1:6 (NIV) ⁶I pray that you may be active in sharing your faith, so that you will have a full understanding of every good thing we have in Christ.
>
> Write out the Life Truth, question, and answer on one side of an index card and the verse on the other side. Keep it in your Bible for the week. Work on it every day individually and as a family. Have it memorized by next week.

According to Philemon 1:6 - What do we need to be active in to have a full understanding of every good thing we have in Christ?

Read Luke 24:45-49; Acts 1:8 What is to be preached to all nations? R_____ and F_____ of sins.
What was God going to send that would clothe them with power? H_____ S_____
What are we supposed to be? God's W_____

Read 2 Timothy 1:7-8 Paul tells Timothy that God gave us a Spirit of P_____.
In verse 8 it tells us to not be
A_____.
Ashamed to do what? T_____ about our L_____.

Read Acts 16:23; 2 Corinthians 6:4,5; 2 Corinthians 11:23-27 Paul tells Timothy to join with him in suffering for the gospel. List four things believers suffered back then?
1.
2.
3.
4.

What persecutions might happen to us today?

Read Luke 21:8-19; 2 Tim. 4:16-18 - What does God promise those who will be arrested for Him?
Luke 21:15 W_____ and
W_____   *2 Tim. 4:17* S_____

Read Matthew 28:18-20 – God's commission for us is to make disciples by T_____ them to O_____
E_____ Christ commanded. What would this look like in our everyday life?

We should share our Life Truths with others to teach them to obey. Using one of the Life Truths write down what you could say to witness to someone: *(Did you know that God's Word says…)*

Based on this LIFE TRUTH what commitments do you need to make to be a better witness? Who will you witness to this week? What will you say? (Keep each other accountable in your Life Group this week)

SELF-GOVERNMENT
LIFE TRUTH # 8
I AM CREATED TO FORGIVE

Each one of us is in desperate need of the forgiveness of God. We have broken God's law and we are deserving of hell. Scripture declares that our sins have separated us from a holy God, but God in His great love, has made a way for us to be forgiven.

*Acts 13:38 (NIV) [38] "Therefore, my brothers, I want you to know that **through Jesus the forgiveness of sins is proclaimed to you**.*

Through Jesus and the sacrifice that He made for us on the cross, we have the possibility of forgiveness. Our hearts should feel as David's did in *Psalm 32:1-2 (NIV) [1] Blessed is he whose transgressions are forgiven, whose sins are covered. [2] Blessed is the man whose sin the LORD does not count against him and in whose spirit is no deceit.*

We must believe in Jesus and make Him the Lord of our lives to be forgiven. *John 3:36 (NIV) [36] Whoever believes in the Son has eternal life, but whoever rejects the Son will not see life, for God's wrath remains on him." Acts 3:19 (NIV) [19] Repent, then, and turn to God, so that your sins may be wiped out, that times of refreshing may come from the Lord,*

When we repent, God takes our sinful record and places it on Christ. He takes Christ's record of righteousness and places it on our record. This is called imputed righteousness. Our sinful record is paid for by Christ's blood and Christ's righteousness is accredited to our account.

Romans 4:23-25 (NIV) [23] The words "it was credited to him" were written not for him alone, [24] but also for us, to whom God will credit righteousness—for us who believe in him who raised Jesus our Lord from the dead. [25] He was delivered over to death for our sins and was raised to life for our justification.

Grace is unmerited favor. It is true forgiveness. We cannot work to earn God's forgiveness or favor. In fact, the opposite is true. He came to die for us on the cross and offer us forgiveness, even though we were enemies of God sinning against Him.

Romans 5:8 (NIV) 8 But God demonstrates his own love for us in this: *While we were still sinners, Christ died for us.*

God reached out to us when we were sinning against Him. He expects us to do the same toward those who are offending us. He not only expects us to forgive; He commands us to forgive! He is so serious about us forgiving others that our salvation is dependent upon it.

In our old nature, we demand our rights and hold grudges. But in our new nature, we forgive others just like Jesus has forgiven us. It is forgiveness that is unmerited and undeserved.

Forgiveness is powerful! Forgiveness is evidence that Christ is in you! Forgiveness is what our world needs to see through the followers of Jesus.

I AM CREATED TO FORGIVE.

When Jesus was teaching His disciples to pray, He gave them the example that we call The Lord's Prayer. Look at what He said in *Matthew 6:9-13 (NIV)* *[9] "This, then, is how you should pray: "'Our Father in heaven, hallowed be your name, [10] your kingdom come, your will be done on earth as it is in heaven. [11] Give us today our daily bread. [12]* **Forgive us our debts, as we also have forgiven our debtors**. *[13] And lead us not into temptation, but deliver us from the evil one.'*

Part of our responsibility when we pray is to make sure that we are forgiving those who offend us. The word debts can be translated *sins*. So the phrase could be better understood in our generation as, "forgive us our sins, as we also have forgiven those who have sinned against us."

As we go through life, people offend us. We get offended when people do not do what we expect them to do. We get offended when people are not sensitive to our needs or wants. We get offended when people do not treat us or those around us right. As Christians, we are to be continually granting forgiveness to those who offend us.

This teaching is throughout the New Testament. Paul writes to remind the believers to forgive in the church at Ephesus and Colosse.

Ephesians 4:32 (NIV) ^{32} *Be kind and compassionate to one another,* ***forgiving each other, just as in Christ God forgave you.***

Colossians 3:12-13 (NIV) ^{12} *Therefore, as God's chosen people, holy and dearly loved, clothe yourselves with compassion, kindness, humility, gentleness and patience.* ^{13} ***Bear with each other and forgive whatever grievances you may have against one another. Forgive as the Lord forgave you.***

We are told to forgive others like Christ forgives us.

How does Christ forgive believers?

1. Jesus died for all of our sin

John 1:29 (NIV) ^{29} *The next day John saw Jesus coming toward him and said, "Look, the Lamb of God,* ***who takes away the sin of the world!*** Is there a sin in your life that Jesus has not died for? No. Jesus died for all sin. If there was a sin in your life that Jesus did not forgive, then you would not be able to enter into heaven. Jesus forgives all sin. We are told to forgive others, "just as in Christ God forgave us." So should we hold grudges? Should we hold a sin over someone's head?   No.

2. Jesus does not bring up our past sins
Psalm 103:11-12 (NIV) [11] For as high as the heavens are above the earth, so great is his love for those who fear him; [12] as far as the east is from the west, **so far has he removed our transgressions from us.**

Romans 4:7-8 (NIV) [7] **"Blessed are they whose transgressions are forgiven, whose sins are covered. [8] Blessed is the man whose sin the Lord will never count against him."** God's compassion for us is immeasurable. His ability to forgive us and not see our past failures is miraculous! My sinful account has been paid for by Christ's sacrifice and Christ's righteousness has accredited my account. When Jesus looks at my record He sees no sin!

Since God treats us with such mercy and compassion, He expects us to do the same for others. Jesus makes it very clear that forgiveness of others is not optional in the life of a believer. He says in *Matthew 6:14-15 (NIV)* [14] *For if you forgive men when they sin against you, your heavenly Father will also forgive you.* [15] ***But if you do not forgive men their sins, your Father will not forgive your sins.***

Some commentaries say that this statement is not saying our salvation is dependent upon the forgiveness of others. I would disagree. This is exactly what Jesus said, *"if we do not forgive men their sins, your father will not forgive your sins."* If God does not forgive our sins, that means we end up in hell. Therefore, our salvation is dependent upon our obedience to God's commands. The ability for us to forgive is evidence that Christ is in us.

As Christians we have the flesh and the Spirit. We are told in *Galatians 5:16 (NIV) ¹⁶ So I say, live by the Spirit, and you will not gratify the desires of the sinful nature.* We have a choice to live by the Spirit and forgive others as Christ forgave us or to live in our flesh and not forgive.

Our forgiveness of others does not earn us our salvation. Christ has done that for us on the cross. But the evidence that Christ is in us, is that we forgive others as He has forgiven us.

UN-FORGIVENESS IS ROOTED IN PRIDE

Pride is undue confidence in ourselves. As our memory verse in Life Truth number 2 points out, there is nothing good that lives in any of us. There is nothing in us to be confident about. Christ reached out to us. If He had not opened our eyes, we would still be blind to salvation or anything righteous. **If anyone does anything righteous, it is because Christ is working through them. If we**

understand anything about God and His Word, it is because the Holy Spirit has revealed it to us. It is not because we have come to understand it on our own.

Paul writes it this way in *I Corinthians 2:14 (NIV)* *[14] The man without the Spirit does not accept the things that come from the Spirit of God, for they are foolishness to him,* **and he cannot understand them,** *because they are spiritually discerned.*

When someone has done something to offend you, they are doing it out of their blindness. You may read this statement and say, *"Oh, no they did not! They knew exactly what they were doing!"* Did they, or were they acting out of their spiritual blindness?

If a blind person bumped into you and spilled hot coffee on you, would you remain angry or have sympathy on them when you realized their condition? Surely, we would have sympathy about their condition and would forgive the offense.

When Jesus was hanging on the cross after he had been severely beaten, mocked, spit upon, and lied about he said this, Luke 23:34 (NIV) [34] ..."**Father, forgive them, for they do not know what they are doing.**"

Jesus said, *"They do not know what they are doing?"* We're not these the men who had been planning a way to kill Jesus? Did the soldiers not know the command of their rulers to kill Jesus? Didn't the crowd have a chance to release Jesus but instead they chose Barabbas? How could Jesus say, *"They did not know what they were doing?"* He was referring to their spiritual blindness. They had been blinded by the ways of Satan and were carrying out his wishes. Jesus talked about this spiritual blindness in *John 9:39-41 (NIV)* [39] *Jesus said, "For judgment I have come into this world, **so that the blind will see and those who see will become blind."** [40] Some Pharisees who were with him heard him say this and asked, "What? Are we blind too?"* [41] *Jesus said, **"If you were blind, you would not be guilty of sin;** but now that you claim you can see, your guilt remains.*

Without Christ in us, we are blind, and we will follow the ways of pride and selfishness. If we are walking with Christ, we will not intentionally offend anyone. *Romans 13:10 (NIV)* [10] **Love does no harm to its neighbor.** *Therefore love is the fulfillment of the law.*

The gospel is offensive to the lost. We have an enemy that we fight against in this world. Those who are offended by the gospel and attack Christians are not doing it on their own. They are following the ways of Satan. They are in spiritual blindness. Stephen understood this spiritual blindness. When the people were stoning him to death, he asked God to forgive them for their actions. *Acts 7:59-60 (NIV)* [59] *While they were stoning him, Stephen prayed, "Lord Jesus, receive my spirit."* [60] *Then he fell on his knees and* *cried out, "**Lord, do not hold this sin against them.**" When he had said this, he fell asleep.*

Stephen was being stoned to death and yet he cried out to God for their forgiveness. When people do smaller offenses toward us, are we willing to cry out to God and ask Him not to hold their sin against them? Are we walking in the Spirit so closely that we love everyone as God does, even the ungodly? Paul talks about this spiritual war in *Ephesians 6:12 (NIV)* *[12] **For our struggle is not against flesh and blood,** but against the rulers, against the authorities, against the powers of this dark world and against the spiritual forces of evil in the heavenly realms.* Our struggle is not against one another, but against Satan and his followers. Those who offend and do harm to one another are walking in darkness. Believers also struggle in this spiritual war and are blinded and offensive at times.

When you are offended intentionally, will you begin to see it as spiritual blindness? Will you say as Stephen did, *"Lord, do not hold this sin against them?"* Many times, we let small offenses drag us down and cause us to act in offensive ways. We need to remember that God has called Christians to a higher standard of love. In our pride, we demand our rights and our revenge for the offense. But in Christ, we are to display only our forgiveness.

Pride keeps a record of wrongs and offenses. Pride points a person's sin out to others. Pride reacts with

insults when insulted. Pride plans ways to get revenge. Pride believes that people can see on their own and is angered when others are "blind".
We are commanded by Christ to love others as Christ has loved us. *John 13:34-35 (NIV)* *[34] "A new command I give you: Love one another. As I have loved you, so you must love one another.* **[35] By this all men will know that you are my disciples, if you love one another."**

Paul describes this kind of Godly love in *I Corinthians 13:1-8 (NIV)* *[1] If I speak in the tongues of men and of angels, but have not love, I am only a resounding gong or a clanging cymbal. [2] If I have the gift of prophecy and can fathom all mysteries and all knowledge, and if I have a faith that can move mountains, but have not love, I am nothing. [3] If I give all I possess to the poor and surrender my body to the flames, but have not love, I gain nothing. [4] Love is patient, love is kind. It does not envy, it does not boast, it is not proud. [5] It is not rude, it is not self-seeking, it is not easily angered,* **it keeps no record of wrongs.** *[6] Love does not delight in evil but rejoices with the truth. [7] It always protects, always trusts, always hopes, always perseveres. [8] Love never fails.*

This kind of love is rooted in forgiveness and in the ability to overlook offenses. *Matthew 5:43-48 (NIV)* *[43] "You have heard that it was said, 'Love your neighbor and hate your enemy.' [44] But I tell you:* **Love your enemies and pray for those who persecute you,** *[45]* **that you may be sons of your Father in heaven.** *He causes his sun to rise on the evil and the good, and sends rain on* *the righteous and the unrighteous. ⁴⁶ If you love those who love you, what reward will you get? Are not even the tax collectors doing that? ⁴⁷ And if you greet only your brothers, what are you doing more than others? Do not even pagans do that? ⁴⁸ Be perfect, therefore, as your heavenly Father is perfect.*

Christians have the ability through Christ to love their enemies. We are told to love enemies who offend us and seek to do us harm. Jesus implies that there is no reward for us if we love only those who love us. Even the pagans, who are spiritually blind, do that.

BIBLICAL SIGNS THAT WE HAVE NOT FORGIVEN

1. Slander

Slander is to speak critically about someone. It is to point out the faults of others in a negative way. A person who slanders others brings out their areas of weakness, not in a prayerful or concerned manner, but in a way that presents the person in a negative light. It is done in a way to elevate their own ability to see and the slandered person's inability to see. People who slander others are spiritually blind and have an unbiblical understanding of God's grace in their own life.

For example, let's look at the life of a homeless man. I could point my finger at him and tell others about all the bad choices he made to get into his situation. Perhaps, he was a drunkard, a thief, or a drug addict. But if I point out his faults, with no concern or understanding of his blindness, I slander him to another. The only reason that I am not the homeless man, inflicted by an addiction or bad times, is by the grace of God. I did not acquire my blessings or understandings on my own ability. God gave me new eyes to see and the strength to defeat such immoralities.

I should look at this homeless man with understanding, compassion, and empathy for his situation and seek to help him in his sinful state. Wouldn't this be the Christ-like thing to do? When I was in a similar state, God came for me the ungodly.

Many times people offend us because of what they said or did. Instead of forgiving them, we slander them to others. What about when someone does not say *"Hi"* to us when we enter into church? Should we tell others about their failure to speak to us? Should we say things like, *"Can you believe so and so did not even speak to me when I came to church?"* No, even in this little offense slander can be committed. We must never slander others, no matter what the offense.

James 4:11 (NIV) [11] **Brothers, do not slander one another.** *Anyone who speaks against his brother or judges him speaks against the law and judges it. When* *you judge the law, you are not keeping it, but sitting in judgment on it.*

Paul writes to the church in Corinth and warns them of specific sins that will keep them out of heaven and slander is one of them. *1 Corinthians 6:9-10 (NIV) ⁹ Do you not know that the wicked will not inherit the kingdom of God? Do not be deceived: Neither the sexually immoral nor idolaters nor adulterers nor male prostitutes nor homosexual offenders ¹⁰ nor thieves nor the greedy nor drunkards **nor slanderers** nor swindlers will inherit the kingdom of God.*

2. Gossip

Gossiping is talking foolishly and spreading rumors. It can also be repeating a rumor and speaking maliciously about someone. *Proverbs 17:9 (NIV) ⁹ **He who covers over an offense promotes love**, but whoever repeats the matter separates close friends.* The phrase "*repeats the matter*" could also be translated gossips. The Scriptures indicate that gossip stirs up a matter and causes division.

*Proverbs 16:28 (NIV) ²⁸ A perverse man stirs up dissension, **and a gossip separates close friends**.*

Proverbs 26:20 (NIV) ²⁰ Without wood a fire goes out; without gossip a quarrel dies down.

When offenses happen, we should not choose sides and cause the separation of close friends. We should not be talking about their sin. We should be fighting for unity and peace. Jesus said, *Matthew 5:9 (NIV) ⁹ Blessed are the peacemakers, for they will be called sons of God.*

Gossiping, like slander, can be done even if you have not been offended, but it usually begins with an offense. If a person is offended, they may call someone to tell them of the offense. The person who hears about the gossip may then in turn call someone else to tell them. They may even add to the offense by pointing out other negative faults of the individual. Gossip spreads the offense and separates relationships.

Gossip causes division and does not promote unity and love. For example, let's say a husband forgets to take out the trash on his way to work. His wife may call a friend to share about her husband's forgetfulness. The friend may ignite the gossip by bringing up old incidents from the past regarding his forgetfulness or even sharing some of her own husband's mistakes. By the time the husband returns home, his wife may be full of anger, ready to lash out at him for many unforgiven offenses. This is not forgiving the offense. Look at what Peter says in, *I Peter 4:8 (NIV) ⁸ Above all, love each other deeply, because love covers over **a multitude of sins**.* The verse says, "love each other deeply" not on a superficial level but deeply as Christ loves us. Love covers over a multitude of sins. Not a few sins but a multitude of sins.

Love each other as you would want to be loved. If you forget to take out the trash, do you want someone calling another and pointing it out? Would you want them discussing your mistakes or failures? The Bible says in, *Proverbs 19:11 (NIV)* *[11] A man's wisdom gives him patience;* **it is to his glory to overlook an offense.** Love is patient with one another and it seeks to do no harm of another. Paul wrote to the church in Corinth that he feared when he visited, they may still be living like the spiritually blind. *2 Corinthians 12:20 (NIV)* *[20]... I fear that there may be quarreling, jealousy, outbursts of anger, factions, slander, gossip, arrogance and disorder.* All of these sins are rooted in pride and a lack of love for one another. We must learn to be forgiving.

3. Malice

Malice is the intent to do harm to another. It is ill will or spitefulness and it is mainly directed towards those who have offended us. We seek to repay the person who has offended us with evil intent. They insulted me, so I will insult them back. Peter tells us to rid ourselves of such things in *1 Peter 2:1 (NIV)* *[1] Therefore, rid yourselves of* **all malice** *and all deceit, hypocrisy, envy, and* **slander of every kind.**
Paul also tells us to get rid of such sin in *Ephesians 4:31 (NIV)* *[31] Get rid of all bitterness, rage and anger, brawling and* **slander,** *along with* **every form of malice.**

Malice has been committed by all of us. It must be destroyed in our sinful nature. When someone insults us, the instinct from our old nature, is to insult them back. When someone does evil towards us, we feel justified in planning how to get even. If someone offends us, we may intentionally give them the cold shoulder and never talk to them again. This is malice and it is not the agape love that God has called us to have.

BIBLICAL SIGNS THAT WE HAVE FORGIVEN

1. We bless when evil is done to us

The Scripture says in *Romans 5:5 (NIV) ⁵ And hope does not disappoint us, because **God has poured out his love into our hearts** by the Holy Spirit, whom he has given us.*

When we are born again, God's love is poured into our hearts. We are then able to love others as Christ loves us. What did Jesus do when people insulted him? *I Peter 2:23 (NIV) ²³ **When they hurled their insults at him, he did not retaliate**; when he suffered, he made no threats. Instead, he entrusted himself to him who judges justly.*

Not only did Jesus give us the example to follow, but He instructed us to do the same. In *I Peter 3:9 (NIV) ⁹ **Do not repay evil with evil or insult with insult,***

but with blessing, *because to this you were called so that you may inherit a blessing.*

We are called to bless those who insult us and do evil against us. Is a cold shoulder a blessing? Is a spiteful word a blessing? Is a cutting remark a blessing? Are there some who we do not have to bless when they offend us? No, we must bless everyone who offends us.

What would happen in our homes if we displayed this kind of love towards one another? What would happen in our church if we displayed this kind of forgiveness and love? What would happen in our community if we blessed those who treated us unfairly?

2. We wash the feet of our offender

Jesus knows all things. He revealed this about himself when he said in, *"Mark 2:8 (NIV) ⁸ Immediately Jesus knew in his spirit that this was what they were thinking in their hearts, and he said to them, "Why are you thinking these things?*

In knowing all things, Jesus also knew that Judas, one of his disciples, was going to betray him. The Bible tells us, in John 13:21, that this troubled him in his spirit. This is also the passage where Jesus washed his disciples' feet. Jesus, the King of Kings and Lord of Lords, knelt down and took the position of a servant and washed the feet of men. Not only did he wash the feet of those who had offended him and sinned against him but he knelt down and washed the feet of the one who would betray him with a kiss. The passage points out that the devil had already prompted Judas to betray Jesus in *John 13:2 (NIV) [2] The evening meal was being served, and the devil had already prompted Judas Iscariot, son of Simon, to betray Jesus.*

Jesus washed the feet of the one he knew would never repent and follow him. He washed the feet of the one who would betray him. The one who would turn him over to authorities to be beaten beyond recognition and then to be crucified on the cross. Jesus was broken in his spirit for Judas because he knew who was behind this offense. The devil was prompting Judas to do this. Judas was blind to the fact that he was a pawn of Satan.

Can we wash the feet of our offenders? Will we kneel down before them and humble ourselves, realizing that life is not about us, but about giving glory to God in all we do? By forgiving others, as Christ has forgiven us, we reveal that we are his children, born not from a natural decent, but born from above.

3. We forgive from the heart

Matthew 18:21-35 (NIV) [21] Then Peter came to Jesus and asked, "Lord, how many times shall I forgive my brother when he sins against me? Up to seven times?" [22] Jesus *answered, "I tell you, not seven times, but seventy-seven times. ^{23} "Therefore, the kingdom of heaven is like a king who wanted to settle accounts with his servants. ^{24} As he began the settlement, a man who owed him ten thousand talents was brought to him. ^{25} Since he was not able to pay, the master ordered that he and his wife and his children and all that he had be sold to repay the debt. ^{26} "The servant fell on his knees before him. 'Be patient with me,' he begged, 'and I will pay back everything.' ^{27} The servant's master took pity on him, canceled the debt and let him go.*

This act of forgiveness by the Master symbolizes the great debt that we owe to God because of our sin. The man owed ten thousand talents. The debt that he owed would be impossible for him to fulfill. In our day, it would be close to 20 million dollars. The greatness of the debt symbolizes the fact that the payment of our debt of sin is impossible as well. The Master took pity on Him and canceled the debt. Just as Christ has paid in full and cancelled our debt!

The parable then takes a downward turn as the servant does not offer others this same kind of mercy. It goes on, *^{28} "But when that servant went out, he found one of his fellow servants who owed him a hundred denarii. He grabbed him and began to choke him. 'Pay back what you owe me!' he demanded. ^{29} "His fellow servant fell to his knees and begged him, 'Be patient with me, and I will pay you back.'*

Notice that the debt that the servant is trying to get from his fellow servant is nowhere near the debt that the Master canceled for him. Isn't this true in our own lives? Jesus has canceled our debt and freed us from hell, yet many times we hold grudges over silly offenses. We see the fellow servant requesting patience, just as the servant himself asked for mercy from the Master. The Master granted mercy and canceled the debt, but look at how the servant responds, *[30] "But he refused. Instead, he went off and had the man thrown into prison until he could pay the debt. [31] When the other servants saw what had happened, they were greatly distressed and went and told their master everything that had happened. [32] "Then the master called the servant in. 'You wicked servant,' he said, 'I canceled all that debt of yours because you begged me to. [33] Shouldn't you have had mercy on your fellow servant just as I had on you?' [34] In anger his master turned him over to the jailers to be tortured, until he should pay back all he owed.*

When the Master found out about the servant's lack of mercy, he treated him with anger and raised the question, *"Shouldn't you have had mercy on your fellow servant just as I had on you?"* The answer is an emphatic, YES! Of course, the servant should have shown mercy on his fellow servant! We read the parable, but do we meditate upon the meaning?

James tells us that judgment without mercy will be shown to anyone who has not been merciful. Are we showing mercy to others? Are we forgiving others when they sin against us? We should be on our knees asking God to love others through us, as He has loved us. The issue is not just on the surface; the issue is with our hearts. We can pretend on the outside that we have forgiven and smile, but it must be real in our hearts. The parable concludes with this statement, [35] *"This is how my heavenly Father will treat each of you **unless you forgive your brother from your heart.**"*

God is serious about his children displaying his character! I AM CREATED TO FORGIVE!

WORKSHEET FOR SELF-GOVERNMENT
LIFE TRUTH # 8
I AM CREATED TO FORGIVE

Question: Does our old nature want to forgive to others?
Answer: No, it does not. We must crucify our old nature and learn to forgive.

> Matthew 6:14-15 (NIV) [14] For if you forgive men when they sin against you, your heavenly Father will also forgive you. [15] But if you do not forgive men their sins, your Father will not forgive your sins.
>
> Write out the Life Truth, question, and answer on one side of an index card and the verse on the other side. Keep it in your Bible for the week. Work on it every day individually and as a family. Have it memorized by next week.

Read Mark 11:25. God forgiving our sins is dependent upon what?
Can we hold anything against anyone?
Forgiveness is a great Biblical truth until we are the one offended. We must forgive others as Christ forgives us. According to 1 John 1:8-10 how does God forgive us when we ask?
What are we reminded of in verses 8 and 10?

Read Ephesians 4:32. Remembering that we are all sinners helps us when we need to forgive someone. Why is this statement true?

Read Romans 12:17-21. When we are offended are we supposed to take revenge? (vs. 19)

What is to be our response to those who have offended us?

Read 1 Peter 3:8-17. According to verse 9 what are we not supposed to do to inherit a blessing?

What are we supposed to do when insulted or when evil has been done to us?

If someone insults us, are we ever justified in insulting them back?　　　　　If we insult someone back, would this be considered doing evil?

Does this principle apply to everyone we know or can we insult our brothers and sisters back?

According to verse 11 and 12 why is not insulting and repaying evil so important?

Read Matthew 18:21-35. Why does Jesus say we must forgive our brother from our heart?

Based on this LIFE TRUTH what commitments do you need to make to forgive others more? How can we better prepare ourselves for the next offense that comes our way, so that we do not repay evil with evil or insult with insult?

SELF-GOVERNMENT
LIFE TRUTH # 9
I AM CREATED TO BE HOLY

Holiness is a characteristic unique to God's nature. It means to be set apart, to be perfect, to be in awe of, and to display awesome power. To understand holiness, we need to understand more about God because God is holy.

In the Book of Revelation, we get a glimpse of God's throne in heaven. As you read the description, try to picture the scene in your own mind. *Revelation 4:1-11 (NIV) ¹ After this I looked, and there before me was a door standing open in heaven. And the voice I had first heard speaking to me like a trumpet said, "Come up here, and I will show you what must take place after this." ² At once I was in the Spirit, and there before me was a throne in heaven with someone sitting on it. ³ And the one who sat there had the appearance of jasper and carnelian. A rainbow, resembling an emerald, encircled the throne. ⁴ Surrounding the throne were twenty-four other thrones, and seated on them were twenty-four elders. They were dressed in white and had crowns of gold on their heads. ⁵ From the throne came flashes of lightning, rumblings and peals of thunder. Before the throne, seven lamps were blazing. These are the seven spirits of God. ⁶ Also before the throne there was what looked like a sea of glass, clear as crystal. In the center, around the throne, were four living creatures, and they were covered with eyes, in front and in back. ⁷ The first living creature was like a lion, the second was like an ox, the third had a face like a man, the fourth was like a flying eagle. ⁸ Each of the four living creatures had six wings and was covered with eyes all around, even under his wings. Day and night they never stop saying: "Holy, holy, holy is the Lord God Almighty, who was, and is, and is to come." ⁹ Whenever the living creatures give glory, honor and thanks to him who sits on the throne and who lives for ever and ever, ¹⁰ the twenty-four elders fall down before him who sits on the throne, and worship him who lives for ever and ever. They lay their crowns before the throne and say: ¹¹ "You are worthy, our Lord and God, to receive glory and honor and power, for you created all things, and by your will they were created and have their being."*

What an awesome sight! How amazing it will be to see God in all his glory! Do you think you might be terrified? Or will you feel unspeakable awe as you are in the presence of Almighty God? Have you ever heard thunder that's made you jump? The Bible says that, *"from the throne came lighting, rumblings, and peals of thunder."*

Can you picture the huge creatures with six wings and eyes everywhere? Did you notice what they say? The Bible says, "<u>Day and night they never stop saying</u>: "<u>Holy, holy, holy</u> is the Lord God Almighty, who was, and is, and is to come." They use the word holy three times meaning that God is not just holy; He is holy,

holy, holy. There is no match or equal to Almighty God.

The 24 elders fall down before this holy God, day and night, and lay their crowns before Him and worship Him saying, *"You are worthy, our Lord and God, to receive glory and honor and power, for you created all things, and by your will they were created and have their being."*

It's hard to imagine such an awesome scene in heaven. Heaven seems like such a foreign place compared to this sinful world. It is God's desire for us to become holy. The more we become holy, the more we look like aliens and strangers to people in this world. Are you living a holy life? Does the world see you as a stranger?

Holiness is hard to describe because it is solely a characteristic of God. It is far more than God being sinless and perfect. It embodies His majesty and His awesome power! The prophet Isaiah had a similar vision of God and His throne in *Isaiah 6:1-5 (NIV)* *[1] In the year that King Uzziah died, I saw the Lord seated on a throne, high and exalted, and the train of his robe filled the temple. [2] Above him were seraphs, each with six wings: With two wings they covered their faces, with two they covered their feet, and with two they were flying. [3] And they were calling to one another: "Holy, holy, holy is the LORD Almighty; the whole earth is full of his glory." [4] At the sound of their voices the doorposts and thresholds shook and the temple was filled with smoke.* ⁵ *"Woe to me!" I cried. "I am ruined! For I am a man of unclean lips, and I live among a people of unclean lips, and my eyes have seen the King, the LORD Almighty."*

The seraphs are similar to the creatures John spoke about in his vision. In both cases, they have six wings and cry out holy, holy, holy. Their repeating of the word holy is to stress God's greatness. There is no equal to God. In verse 5, Isaiah describes how he felt being in the presence of Holy God, "Woe to me!" He cries, "I am ruined!"

John describes his reaction when he comes into the presence of the Holy One. *Revelation 1:17 (NIV)* [17] *When I saw him, I fell at his feet as though dead.* God's perfection, majesty, power, and his holiness cause us to realize our sinfulness and total depravity. Holiness encompasses justice and when a wrong has been committed punishment must follow. God would not be holy if He did not punish sin.

God is all knowing and therefore knows everything about everyone. He knows our words, actions, and even our thoughts. With this knowledge, he can make righteous judgments. It is because of his holiness that justice must be carried out. When sinful man enters into His presence, justice begins. God's holiness causes man to say like Isaiah, "Woe is me! I am ruined!"

The amazing thing about our Holy God is that He wants to have a relationship with us, even though we are sinners. When God created Adam and Eve in the Garden of Eden, the Bible says that God walked with them and spent time with them. But that relationship changed, when Adam and Eve ate the forbidden fruit. It forced God to expel them from the garden. God made the first sacrifice for their sin when He killed an animal and made for them clothes of skin. (Gen 3:21).

Throughout history, this holy God has desired to spend time with His creations. In the Old Testament God told Moses to build Him a sanctuary a place for Him to dwell. *Exodus 25:8 (NIV) ⁸ "Then have them make a sanctuary for me, and I will dwell among them.* In the previous chapter, it tells us that Moses and many others got a vision of the throne room in heaven, like John and Isaiah did. *Exodus 24:9-12 (NIV) ⁹ Moses and Aaron, Nadab and Abihu, and the seventy elders of Israel went up ¹⁰ and saw the God of Israel. Under his feet was something like a pavement made of sapphire, clear as the sky itself. ¹¹ But God did not raise his hand against these leaders of the Israelites; they saw God, and they ate and drank. ¹² The LORD said to Moses, "Come up to me on the mountain and stay here, and I will give you the tablets of stone, with the law and commands I have written for their instruction."*

The tablets of stone are the Ten Commandments that all nations are to follow. They teach us how to be holy. Moses was told to build the earthly tabernacle exactly like the one in heaven. *Exodus 25:9*

(NIV) ⁹ *Make this tabernacle and all its furnishings exactly like the pattern I will show you.*

In the Old Testament, this tabernacle is how God dwelt among the people. The tabernacle had three main sections. Each section contained special, sacred objects.

1. The Courtyard

The Courtyard was the main access to the tabernacle. The wide gate was the place where ancient Israelites would bring their sacrifices and offerings. Within the courtyard, the priests would offer sacrifices at the bronze altar. There was also a bronze laver, in which the priests could cleanse themselves to be ritually clean.

2. The Holy Place

The Holy Place housed three important objects for the service of the tabernacle: the golden lamp, the table of the bread of the presence, and the altar of incense. The priests performed daily tasks inside the Holy Place: they had to keep the lamps burning, offer incense twice a day, and bring fresh bread weekly to the table.

3. The Holy of Holies also called the Most Holy Place

The Holy of Holies was a unique place. The Ark of the Covenant was in this room. God's very presence dwelt in the Holy of Holies. Only the high priest could enter this room once a year. It was protected by a cloud of burning incense. The most important celebration in the Jewish calendar, the Day of Atonement, had its climax in the Holy of Holies. The Holy of Holies was the place where the high priest would offer God the blood of a sacrificed animal to atone for the peoples' sin.

When it was time for the high priest to enter into the Holy of Holies, he had to perform sacrifices and rituals to prepare himself to be in the presence of God. If the high priest entered the room without obeying God's requirements for entering into His presence, he would die. As a safeguard for the other priests, he would tie a rope around his waist. The rope was their way to pull the dead high priest out without entering into God's holy presence unworthily.

The Book of Hebrews talks about this tabernacle. *Hebrews 9:1-8 (NIV) [1] Now the first covenant had regulations for worship and also an earthly sanctuary. [2] A tabernacle was set up. In its first room were the lampstand, the table and the consecrated bread; this was called the Holy Place. [3] Behind the second curtain was a room called the Most Holy Place, [4] which had the golden altar of incense and the gold-covered Ark of the Covenant.*

This ark contained the gold jar of manna, Aaron's staff that had budded, and the stone tablets of the covenant. [5] Above the ark were the cherubim of the Glory, overshadowing the atonement cover. But we cannot discuss these things in detail now. [6] When everything had been arranged like this, the priests entered regularly into the outer room to carry on their ministry. [7] But only the high priest entered the inner room, and that only once a year, and never without blood, which he offered for himself and for the sins the people had committed in ignorance. [8] The Holy Spirit was showing by this that the way into the Most Holy Place had not yet been disclosed as long as the first tabernacle was still standing.

The Old Testament reveals the holiness of God and how man must respect God and His presence. The nation of Israel had to offer sacrifices to atone for their sins in order to have the presence of God in their midst. They also had to have a right attitude and a pure heart. However, when Jesus came, he opened the door for everyone to enter into the Holy of Holies.

When Christ came, he shed His blood and became the perfect sacrifice to atone for our sins. The Scriptures declare that Jesus' blood was taken to the throne in heaven, not the earthly tabernacle, but to the throne of God. Hebrews 9:11-14 (NIV) [11] *When Christ came as high priest of the good things that are already here, he went through the greater and more perfect tabernacle that is not man-made, that is to say, not a part of this creation.* [12] *He did not enter by means of the blood of goats and calves; but he entered the Most Holy Place once for all by his own blood, having obtained eternal redemption. [13] The blood of goats and bulls and the ashes of a heifer sprinkled on those who are ceremonially unclean sanctify them so that they are outwardly clean. [14] How much more, then, will the blood of Christ, who through the eternal Spirit offered himself unblemished to God, cleanse our consciences from acts that lead to death, so that we may serve the living God!*

All of us, through Christ, can have access to the most holy place. Prior to Christ, only the high priest and those God allowed could enter into his presence. *Hebrews 10:19-22 (NIV) [19] Therefore, brothers, since we have confidence to enter the Most Holy Place by the blood of Jesus, [20] by a new and living way opened for us through the curtain, that is, his body, [21] and since we have a great priest over the house of God, [22] let us draw near to God with a sincere heart in full assurance of faith, having our hearts sprinkled to cleanse us from a guilty conscience and having our bodies washed with pure water.*
Christ's sacrifice has made us holy. Our debt has been paid. Through Jesus, we have access to be in the presence of Almighty God.
The book of Matthew says that when Christ died, the curtain in the temple was torn from top to bottom. God tore the curtain, making a way for us to have access into the Holy of Holies. The Bible says in *Matthew 27:50-51 (NIV) [50] And when Jesus had cried out again in a loud voice, he gave up his spirit. [51] At that*

moment the curtain of the temple was torn in two from top to bottom.

Before Jesus died, he talked to his disciples about heaven. He said in *John 14:1-5 (NIV)* [1] *"Do not let your hearts be troubled. Trust in God; trust also in me.* [2] *In my Father's house are many rooms; if it were not so, I would have told you. I am going there to prepare a place for you.* [3] *And if I go and prepare a place for you, I will come back and take you to be with me that you also may be where I am.* [4] *You know the way to the place where I am going."* [5] *Thomas said to him, "Lord, we don't know where you are going, so how can we know the way?"*

Thomas wondered how they would find this amazing place with many rooms. How would they get there? Jesus answered him by sharing Jewish knowledge of the Temple.

By the porch, near the stairs, in the direction the Holy of Holies, was a door. The first doorway was called *The Life*. The second doorway was called *The Truth*. The third, which was the entryway into the Holy of Holies, was called *The Way*. Jesus said in *John 14:6 (NIV)* [6] *"I am the way and the truth and the life. No one comes to the Father except through me."* It is through Jesus alone that we have access to the God who dwells in the Holy of Holies. Without His sacrifice and His atonement for our sins, we would perish in the presence of Almighty God.

When we believe in Jesus, and make Him our Lord, we are given eternal life. This is the first curtain. It shows that we have chosen to enter into the presence of God. The next curtain is the truth. When we accept Jesus, we are called to follow Him and walk in obedience to His commands. His commands teach us how to be holy. As we obey the teachings of Christ, we become holy as God is holy. The last curtain is the way. This is the curtain that gives us entry into the Holy of Holies. Those who enter through the first two curtains are able to enter through the last curtain and live with God forever. These people are the overcomers.

The life curtain is when we are born again and we receive the Holy Spirit. We then become the temple for God's Spirit. We are freed from our sins. We are no longer bound to sin and have the ability to be holy. The truth shows us the pathway to follow and leads us to the Most Holy Place.

God's desire, since creation, has been to spend time with his children. His holiness, however, demands that there be a way for us to be in His presence without being destroyed by our sin. The only way that gives us access to Holy God is through Christ Jesus.

When this world has ended and Christ makes the new heaven and the new earth listen to what he says, *Revelation 21:1-8 (NIV) [1] Then I saw a new heaven and a new earth, for the first heaven and the first earth had passed away, and there was no longer any sea. ² I saw the Holy City, the new Jerusalem, coming down out of heaven from God, prepared as a bride beautifully dressed for her husband. ³ And I heard a loud voice from the throne saying,* **"Now the dwelling of God is with men, and he will live with them. They will be his people, and God himself will be with them and be their God.** *⁴ He will wipe every tear from their eyes. There will be no more death or mourning or crying or pain, for the old order of things has passed away." ⁵ He who was seated on the throne said, "I am making everything new!" Then he said, "Write this down, for these words are trustworthy and true." ⁶ He said to me: "It is done. I am the Alpha and the Omega, the Beginning and the End. To him who is thirsty I will give to drink without cost from the spring of the water of life.*

Heaven is going to be a place where we will dwell with God forever. God himself will be able to dwell with us because of what Christ did in taking our punishment for sin. The Scripture goes on to declare who will be his people in this awesome place.⁷ *He who overcomes will inherit all this, and I will be his God and he will be my son.*

This passage then concludes with those who will not be able to dwell with God forever in heaven.
⁸ But the cowardly, the unbelieving, the vile, the murderers, the sexually immoral, those who practice magic arts, the idolaters and all liars–their place will be in the fiery lake of burning sulfur. This is the second death."

The holy God has made a way for us to dwell with him forever, but not everyone will be able to enter. Who will be able to enter? Only the overcomers and the holy will be able to enter. *Hebrews 12:14 (NIV)* [14] *Make every effort to live in peace with all men and* **to be holy; without holiness no one will see the Lord.** When we repent, and call upon Jesus as Lord, the Holy Spirit resides within us. We receive the same Spirit that dwelt in the Holy of Holies. *I Corinthians 6:19-20 (NIV)* [19] *Do you not know that your body is a temple of the Holy Spirit, who is in you, whom you have received from God? You are not your own;* [20] *you were bought at a price. Therefore honor God with your body.* Believers are the tabernacle for God. We have a responsibility to be holy because we house God's Holy Spirit. *I Peter 1:15* [15] *But just as he who called you is holy,* **so be holy <u>in all</u> you do**; [16] *for it is written:* **"Be holy, because I am holy."**

It is a very serious matter to be holy. We disgrace God when we act in sinful ways. Scriptures warn us from acting in sinful defiant ways.

Hebrews 10:26-31 (NIV) [26] *If we <u>deliberately</u> keep on sinning after we have received the knowledge of the truth, no sacrifice for sins is left,* [27] *but only a fearful expectation of judgment and of raging fire that will consume the enemies of God.* [28] *Anyone who rejected the law of Moses died without mercy on the testimony of two or three witnesses.* [29] *How much more severely do you think a man deserves to be punished who has trampled the Son of God under foot, who has treated as an unholy thing the* *blood of the covenant that sanctified him, and who has insulted the Spirit of grace? [30] For we know him who said, "It is mine to avenge; I will repay," and again, "The Lord will judge his people." [31] It is a dreadful thing to fall into the hands of the living God.*

The key word is <u>deliberately</u>. God has called us to be sanctified. The definition of sanctification is to be made holy. It also means to be set apart. God desires for his people to begin a process of being made holy. Once we've accepted Jesus, we should be progressing towards holiness with each passing year. This is the process of sanctification. If you are no more holy than when you first accepted Jesus, you are not entering through the curtain called truth. We must study the Scriptures daily, apply them to our lives, and continually ask the Holy Spirit to enable us to be holy.

Here are four ways that we need to be holy

1. Be perfect

Jesus said in *Matthew 5:48 (NIV)* [48] *Be perfect, therefore, as your heavenly Father is perfect.* Have you ever heard the phrase that *no one is perfect?* This phrase is used many times to justify sin. By being holy, we are to be perfect, not just perfect based on a human standard, but perfect, *"as your heavenly father is perfect."* How perfect is God? Does He tell white lies and justify sin? Being perfect means to stop justifying our sins; stop telling the white lies; stop pretending that you don't know any better; stop saying to yourself that everybody does it; stop believing the lie that "good" people go to heaven.

The world lowers the standard of perfection and gives people a false assurance that they do not need to be holy to enter into heaven. Scriptures declare otherwise. *I Thessalonians 4:3-8 (NIV) ³ It is God's will that you should be sanctified: that you should avoid sexual immorality; ⁴ that each of you should learn to control his own body in a way that is holy and honorable, ⁵ not in passionate lust like the heathen, who do not know God; ⁶ and that in this matter no one should wrong his brother or take advantage of him.* **The Lord will punish men for all such sins, as we have already told you and warned you.** *⁷* **For God did not call us to be impure, but to live a holy life**. *⁸ Therefore, he who rejects this instruction does not reject man but God, who gives you his Holy Spirit.*

When we come into the presence of the Holy One, we better be ready. Are you ready? Are you living in defiant sin? Are you justifying your sin and thinking that it is no big deal? Repent and turn to God so that your sins may be wiped away.

Who was able to enter into the Holy of Holies only one time each year? The high priest. Look at what Peter says about us, *I Peter 2:9 (NIV) ⁹ But you are a* **chosen people, a royal priesthood, a holy nation,** *a people belonging to God, that you may declare the praises of him who called you out of darkness into his* *wonderful light.* The priests had all kinds of priestly duties and they had special articles to wear.

On his head he wore a turban with a gold plate across the front with an inscription. *Exodus 28:36-37 (NIV) [36] "Make a plate of pure gold and engrave on it as on a seal: HOLY TO THE LORD. [37] Fasten a blue cord to it to attach it to the turban; it is to be on the front of the turban.* We are to be a kingdom of priests and a holy nation. We are to be like the priests who had "HOLY TO THE LORD" written across their foreheads. Although we do not have to wear gold plates, our actions should reveal that we are filled with the spirit of the holy God everywhere we go.

2. Be set apart

Holiness is separation from all that is common and unclean. But who gets to decide what is common and unclean? What may be unclean to you might be perfectly acceptable to me. How can we decide what is moral and what is immoral? God has given us the Bible to govern our lives by. There is no other standard necessary.

Ephesians 5:1-7 (NIV) [1] Be imitators of God, therefore, as dearly loved children [2] and live a life of love, just as Christ loved us and gave himself up for us as a fragrant offering and sacrifice to God. [3] **But among you there must not be <u>even a hint</u>** *of sexual immorality, or of any kind of impurity, or of greed, because* **these are improper for God's holy people.** *[4] Nor should there be* *obscenity, foolish talk or coarse joking, which are out of place, but rather thanksgiving. ⁵ For of this you can be sure: No immoral, impure or greedy person–such a man is an idolater–has any inheritance in the kingdom of Christ and of God. ⁶ Let no one deceive you with empty words, for because of such things God's wrath comes on those who are disobedient. ⁷* **Therefore do not be partners with them.**

The world's ways are opposing to God. The world's music, movies, philosophies, and standards do not meet the standards that believers are called to live by. We are told not to be partners with the disobedient. An area the church needs to be very concerned about in today's generation is our current partnership with "Hollywood". I use the term "Hollywood" as a general reference to current music, movies, and television programs. How many worldly songs, movies, or television shows have immorality in them? Most of them. Almost every "Hollywood" movie today has some type of obscenity. The passage in Ephesians clearly states what the disobedient do. They are sexually immoral, impure, and speak obscenities. Hollywood makes their money from those who partner with them and buy their products. We cannot partner with the disobedient if we want to be holy or set apart. We must stop partnering with the disobedient as it is only bringing more judgment upon ourselves and our nation.

To be set apart is to be different from the world; so different that you look like an alien or stranger here. When we get our new nature, we begin to walk in holiness. We are to stop acting like the world. We are to stop speaking like the world. We are to stop going to the wild parties and participating in what the disobedient do. *I Peter 2:11 (NIV)* *¹¹ **Dear friends, I urge you, as aliens and strangers in the world, to abstain from sinful desires, which war against your soul.***

Being set apart is hard work. It creates a battle within us. Our flesh desires to sin, but the Holy Spirit within us has the power to enable us to walk in righteousness. Being set apart means getting on your knees and asking God for help. He will free you from your sinful desires and addictions. It also means to stop hanging out with those who are causing you to sin. If you have a problem with alcoholism, you won't defeat it by hanging out in a bar with people who drink. Break free of them and be separate! Find new friends, at church, and begin to conquer your addictions.

Wouldn't it be odd to see a priest hanging out in a bar, at a wild party, with a group of people cursing, or at an immoral movie? If it is out of place for a priest of God, it should be out of place for anyone who calls themselves a Christian. We are the kingdom of priests and the Christ-like character we display to others must to be taken very seriously.

3. Display God's power

As we become set apart from sin, we display God's holiness and power to the world. When Christ died on the cross for us, he defeated all sin and cleansed our consciousness from acts that lead to death. Jesus has set us free from sin! We are no longer bound to obey sin's passions. We can walk away from every addiction.

Romans 6:11-14 (NIV) [11] In the same way, count yourselves dead to sin but alive to God in Christ Jesus. [12] **Therefore do not let sin reign in your mortal body so that you obey its evil desires.** *[13] Do not offer the parts of your body to sin, as instruments of wickedness, but rather offer yourselves to God, as those who have been brought from death to life; and offer the parts of your body to him as instruments of righteousness. [14] For sin shall not be your master, because you are not under law, but under grace.*

If you are struggling with an addiction, don't hide it and live in shame. Confess it to a trusted believer in Christ and begin to ask God to help you be an overcomer. The world needs to see a powerful church; full of sinners who have been set free. The church seems to be a "fake" place where people pretend to have it all together, but behind the scenes we are full of all kinds of addictions and shame. The people of God need to be declaring:

- *"I once was an alcoholic, but now I have been set free!"*
- *"I once was addicted to pornography, but now I have been set free!"*
- *"I once was full of guilt and shame, but Christ has given me peace and joy!"*
- *"I once was full of bitterness and anger, but Christ has enabled me to forgive!"*

Our testimony is not only that Christ has set us free, but that He desires to set everyone free!

4. Keep your eyes on the heavenly city

Have you noticed all the sin and pain in this world? Our flesh loves this world and all of its indulgences, but the spirit within us is calling us to a better place. A place with no more school shootings, no more harming children, no more terrorists, no more crying, and no more pain. To be holy, we must take our eyes off this world and remain focused on the heavenly city. The great people of faith are described in *Hebrews 11:13-16 (NIV)* *¹³ All these people were still living by faith when they died. They did not receive the things promised; they only saw them and welcomed them from a distance.* ***And they admitted that they were aliens and strangers on earth.*** *¹⁴* ***People who say such things show that they are looking for a country of their own.*** *¹⁵* ***If they had been thinking of the country they had left, they would have had*** *opportunity to return. [16] Instead, they were longing for a better country—a heavenly one. Therefore God is not ashamed to be called their God, for he has prepared a city for them.*

Later on, it says in Hebrews 13:14 (NIV) *[14] For here we do not have an enduring city,* **but we are looking for the city that is to come.**

Remember the descriptions from the throne? What were the living creatures doing? What were the elders doing? They were all worshiping Jesus! They were humbling themselves before the Holy One. They were singing, "Holy, holy, holy is the Lord God Almighty." They were bowing before Him and casting their crowns at His feet. This is how all of us need to come before the One who is worthy of glory, honor, and praise. If we do this, asking Him for forgiveness and strength to obey, He will enable us to be holy, as He is Holy.

When you see the awesome throne of the Holy One and the great beasts crying out holy, holy, holy; will you be ready? Are you ready now? Are you being holy and living as God has called you to?

I AM CREATED TO BE HOLY

WORKSHEET FOR SELF-GOVERNMENT
LIFE TRUTH # 9
I AM CREATED TO BE HOLY

Question: Does our old nature want to be holy?
Answer: No, it does not. We must crucify our old nature and learn to be holy.

> I Peter 1:14-15 (NIV) [14] As obedient children, do not conform to the evil desires you had when you lived in ignorance. [15] But just as he who called you is holy, so be holy in all you do;
>
> Write out the Life Truth, question, and answer on one side of an index card and the verse on the other side. Keep it in your Bible for the week. Work on it every day individually and as a family. Have it memorized by next week.

Read I Peter 1:13-16. According to verse 15 how often are we to be holy?

What are the five things, from verses 13 and 14, that we need to do in order to be holy?

Read 2 Corinthians 6:14 -7:1. What does it mean to not be yoked with unbelievers? (Note: To be yoked is to be linked together and headed in the same direction)

We are told to touch no unclean thing in verse 17. How do we know what is clean or unclean? (Hint: Life Truth # 1)

According to these verses how could things like music, movies, television, and books contaminate your body and spirit?
Phil 4:8 and Prov 4:23 -
1 Cor. 6:18,19 -

Read Ephesians 5:1-7. According to this passage the wrath of God comes on who? (vs.6)
 This passage describes what the disobedient do. List two ways.

Verse 7 says that we are not to be partners with the disobedient. How could someone be partners with the disobedient and support their immoralities?

Read 2 Peter 3:3-14. What will the scoffers say in the last days?

According to verse 9 why is God patient with us?

 According to verse 10 -12 the coming of Christ will bring about what?

Since everything will be destroyed what kind of people ought we to be?

What are believers to be looking forward to?

Based on this LIFE TRUTH what commitments do you need to make to be more holy? Being holy means being perfect, being set apart, displaying God's power in us, and always keeping our eyes on the heavenly city. Which do to you need to work on most and why?

SELF-GOVERNMENT
LIFE TRUTH # 10
I AM CREATED TO WORK

We are told in the Scriptures that we cannot work to earn our salvation. *Ephesians 2:8-9 (NIV)* *⁸ For it is by grace you have been saved, through faith– and this not from yourselves, it is the gift of God–* **⁹ not by works,** *so that no one can boast.* We cannot do enough works to earn God's favor or to repay our sins. **Salvation comes by grace through faith alone!** We must trust in what Jesus did for us on the cross. He offers salvation for all who believe and make Him their Lord.

Salvation gives us a new nature. It is through our new nature that we have works to do. **Works do not save us but they are the evidence that we are saved!** Our faith is made complete by what we do after salvation.

The Bible speaks about Abraham in *James 2:22-24 (NIV)* *²² You see that his faith and his actions were working together, and* **his faith was made complete by what he did**. *²³ And the scripture was fulfilled that says, "Abraham believed God, and it was credited to him as righteousness," and he was called God's friend.*

The Bible makes it clear that a person is made complete by what he does.

If we performed works to **earn** our salvation, we would fall terribly short of the standard, which is holiness. It is when we understand that we are saved, forgiven, and loved by God that we produce "good works" **because of Christ in us**. Through faith we allow Christ to work through us. God enlightens and empowers us to: deny ourselves, pick up our cross, crucify the flesh, and live by the Spirit.

The verse that follows the scripture that says we are saved by grace through faith alone is *Ephesians 2:10 (NIV)* *¹⁰ For we are God's workmanship,* **created in Christ Jesus to do good works,** *which God prepared in advance for us to do.*

The Bible also warns us that we will be judged based on our works. *Revelation 22:12 (NIV)* *¹² "Behold, I am coming soon! My reward is with me, and* **I will give to everyone according to what he has done.**

We have no excuse not to fulfill the works that God has prepared in advance for us to do. He has given us all that we need to accomplish the tasks that He has for us to do. You will not be able to say on the Day of Judgment, *"I didn't know what you wanted me to do."* You won't be able to say, *"I wasn't given the right "tools" to complete the task."* God's Word and the Holy Spirit are the right tools.

Philippians 2:12-13 (NIV) *¹² Therefore, my dear friends, as you have always obeyed–not only in my presence, but now much more in my absence–***continue to work out** *your salvation with fear and trembling,* [13] **_for it is God_** _who works in you_ *to will and to act according to his good purpose.*

So how do I know what works I am to accomplish? *2 Timothy 3:16-17 (NIV)* [16] *All Scripture is God-breathed and is useful for teaching, rebuking, correcting and training in righteousness,* [17] **so that the man of God may be thoroughly equipped for every good work.** If we fail to know the Scriptures and apply them to our lives, we will fail to fulfill the good works that God has prepared in advance for us to do.

WORKING IS GOD'S INTENTION FOR MAN

From the very beginning of man, it was God's intention that we should work. *Genesis 2:15 (NIV)* [15] *The LORD God took the man and put him in the Garden of Eden* **to work it and take care of it**. We are the stewards of God's creation. We have responsibilities to fulfill for God. The day is coming when we will be judged on how we have worked for God.

When Adam and Eve sinned, the responsibility to work did not change. The work became harder, however, because of their sin.

Genesis 3:23 (NIV) [23] *So the LORD God banished him from the Garden of Eden* **to work the ground** *from which he had been taken.* After the fall of man, the ground became cursed. Our toil in working the ground would now produce sweat.

*Genesis 3:17-19 (NIV) ⁱ⁷ To Adam he said, "Because you listened to your wife and ate from the tree about which I commanded you, 'You must not eat of it,' "**Cursed is the ground** because of you; **through painful toil** you will eat of it all the days of your life. ¹⁸ It will produce thorns and thistles for you, and you will eat the plants of the field. ¹⁹ By the sweat of your brow you will eat your food until you return to the ground, since from it you were taken; for dust you are and to dust you will return."*

Man **working** has been God's intention since the very beginning. He plans for us to **work** in heaven, as well. Those who accept Jesus as their Lord, completing the works that God has prepared for them to do, will enter into the new heaven and the new earth. The Scriptures teach that we will continue to serve God and have responsibilities in heaven.

*Revelation 22:3 (NIV) ³ No longer will there be any curse. The throne of God and of the Lamb will be in the city, and **his servants will serve him**.*

*Matthew 25:21 (NIV) ²¹ "His master replied, 'Well done, good and faithful servant! You have been faithful with a few things; **I will put you in charge of many things**. Come and share your master's happiness!'*

The Garden of Eden, where God dwelt with man, will be renewed in the new heaven and the new earth.

However, God's intentions for us to serve Him and to work will continue. We will all have specific responsibilities and things to take care of.

Throughout the New Testament, we are told to work and that our godly works bring glory to God. *Matthew 5:16 (NIV) ⁱ⁶ In the same way, let your light shine before men, that they may see your **good deeds** and praise your Father in heaven.*

*Colossians 1:10 (NIV) ¹⁰ And we pray this in order that you may live a life worthy of the Lord and may please him in every way: **bearing fruit in every good work,** growing in the knowledge of God,*

*Hebrews 10:24 (NIV) ²⁴ And let us consider how we may spur one another on toward love and **good deeds.***

*1 Peter 2:12 (NIV) ¹² Live such good lives among the pagans that, though they accuse you of doing wrong, <u>they may see your **good deeds** and glorify God</u> on the day he visits us.*

Everything we do should be looked at as a spiritual responsibility. We can better understand our responsibilities for work by breaking it down into two categories: earthly and heavenly. Earthly responsibilities are the works we need to do here while we live on this earth. Heavenly responsibilities refer to the building of God's kingdom here on earth as well.

Earthly work

I want to stress again that even though we are calling these responsibilities earthly, they still have heavenly consequences and rewards. Even in our earthly responsibilities, we must be doing them to bring glory to God. Paul says it this way in *Colossians 3:17 (NIV)* *17 And whatever you do, whether in word or deed, do it all in the name of the Lord Jesus, giving thanks to God the Father through him.*

From our Life Truth: We are Created to be Holy, we learned that we are to be holy in all that we do. Peter goes on to say in *1 Peter 1:17 (NIV)* **17 Since you call on a Father who judges each man's work impartially,** *live your lives as strangers here in reverent fear.* We are to be very concerned with the fact that God will be judging our work impartially and according to the standard of holiness. Even in our earthly responsibilities, God will be judging us.

1. We are to provide for our daily necessities

God told Adam that by the sweat of his own brow, he is to be providing for his own needs. *Genesis 3:19 (NIV)* **19 By the sweat of your brow you will eat your food** *until you return to the ground, since from it you were taken; for dust you are and to dust you will return."*

This does not mean that we are to all be farmers or have our own gardens. It does mean that we are to work and provide for our own needs. We are to work for our own food and do this until we return to the ground. God's design in society is that we each do our part in earning the bread that we eat. When you work at job to earn money, and then you go to a store to buy bread to eat, you are fulfilling one of God's responsibilities.

Paul told Titus to teach the churches to do this in *Titus 3:14 (NIV) ¹⁴ Our people must learn to **devote themselves to doing what is good, in order that they may provide for daily necessities and not live unproductive lives.*** We must devote ourselves to providing for our daily necessities. We are not to live unproductive lives.

The fourth commandment of the Ten Commandments is: Remember the Sabbath and keep it holy. But the first part of the fourth commandment is that we are to work. *Exodus 20:9-10 (NIV) ⁹ Six days you shall labor and do all your work, ¹⁰ but the seventh day is a Sabbath to the LORD your God. On it you shall not do any work, neither you, nor your son or daughter, nor your manservant or maidservant, nor your animals, nor the alien within your gates.*

Remember that sin brought the consequences of hard work. Because of sin, we cannot walk in the Garden of Eden and pick the food we want to eat. We must work by the sweat of our brow to earn the bread we eat. We must provide for our own daily necessities as part of the earthly work that God has called us to do.

It is a grievous sin to God when His people do not work to earn the bread that they eat. God's people are not to be dependent upon anyone. *I Thessalonians 4:11-12 (NIV) ⁱⁱ Make it your ambition to lead a quiet life, to mind your own business and* **to work with your hands***, just as we told you, ¹² so that your daily life may win the respect of outsiders and* **so that you will not be dependent on anybody.**

"To work with your own hands" is not a literal reference to the fact that we need to be using our hands to earn our daily necessities. It means that we are to use whatever gift God has given us to earn a living. Some people may be gifted farmers and work the ground to grow their own food and food to sell to others. Some may use their hands to work in a factory on an assembly line. Some may sit at a desk and use their gift in math to be an accountant. Some may use their gift to preach and teach the Word of God. These are just a few examples of work that would be considered "using their own hands" to earn daily necessities.

When Jesus sent the disciples out to minister the gospel he told them, *Luke 10:5-7 (NIV) ⁵ "When you enter a house, first say, 'Peace to this house.' ⁶ If a man of peace is there, your peace will rest on him; if not, it will return to you. ⁷ Stay in that house,* **eating and drinking** *whatever they give you, for the worker deserves his wages.*

When we are faithfully working hard, even if it is not directly related to earning the bread we eat, we are fulfilling God's purpose to be self-supportive.

To be dependent upon someone is for them to be providing for your daily necessities. We are told in 1 Thessalonians 4:12 not to be dependent upon anyone. To be dependent upon someone is to expect them to meet your daily necessities. The rule to work and provide for your daily necessities is specifically for those who are able to work. An infant or child would not be responsible for their daily necessities. A person who is physically unable to provide for their daily necessities is not expected by God to fulfill this rule. **If a person is unable to work, it is a family government or church government issue. It is never a civil government issue.** Welfare from the civil government is not God's design in the institutions. As we repent and return to God's Word as the only source that governs us, we must begin to start a reformation to get people off government assistance programs.

God expects a person who is able to provide for their own necessities to work. A person who is able to work and does not provide for their own necessities is sinning. The Bible calls this idleness. Jesus commands the church not to be idle in

2 Thessalonians 3:6-12 (NIV) **[6] In the name of the Lord Jesus Christ, we command you,** *brothers, to keep away from every brother who is idle and does not live according to the teaching you received from us.* [7] *For you yourselves know how you ought to follow our example. We were not idle when we were with you,* [8] <u>*nor did we eat anyone's food without paying for it*</u>*. On the contrary, we worked night and day,* <u>*laboring and toiling so that we would not be a burden to any of you*</u>*.* [9] *We did this, not because we do not have the right to such help, but in order to make ourselves a model for you to follow.* [10] *For even when we were with you, we gave you this rule:* **"If a man will not work, he shall not eat."** [11] *We hear that some among you are idle. They are not busy; they are busybodies.* [12] **Such people we command and urge in the Lord Jesus Christ to settle down and earn the bread they eat.**

The Scriptures are very clear that we are to labor and toil to earn the bread we eat. When it says that we are to keep away from *"every brother who is idle,"* it is referring to people who call themselves Christians and are dependent upon others for their daily necessities. If a person is a Christian and is able to work, but they do not, we are told to keep away from them. The goal is not to shun people. It is to awaken them to the seriousness of the command to work. If we teach them to go out and earn the bread they eat, and they refuse, then we must live by the command, *"If you do not work you do not eat."* The command is that we do not help "brothers" who are able to work and refuse to. This would include a

church's assistance to help pay bills or to help buy groceries. Remember, this command applies only to those who are able to work but do not.
If they are on any assistance, whether it is from the government, churches, relatives, or any other source, we are commanded to keep away from them if they refuse to work.

If you are able to work and you do not, but you receive aid from the government or any other source, it is a sin. This is an example of an unproductive life. This is a person who is not earning the bread they eat. The government is not responsible to take care of your daily necessities. It is the responsibility of the individual, the family, and the church.

Someone who is able to work and is receiving aid instead, needs to begin praying and asking God to forgive them, just as they would any other sin in their life. They also need to seriously begin looking for a job, and taking the job the Lord sends their way, no matter how menial the job may seem.

Whenever we sin, we are good at justifying our sin. We like to make excuses for our sin. Someone receiving aid might say, *"If I work I will not make as much as I am receiving now."* The issue is not how much you are receiving now; the issue is that you are to earn the bread that you eat. If you follow the principles of God's Word by becoming an honest hard worker, you will advance in your pay scale. God is our provider. He will give us what we need, but we are responsible to obey him.

The civil government should not be providing for people's daily necessities. This is out of the jurisdiction of what God established for them to do. Many people today are on welfare in America. This is not what God intended. If you are unable to work and provide for your daily needs, God has established a plan for you. If the civil government is not responsible for those who are unable to work, then who is?

2. We are to provide for our families

The family is the first institution that should be taking care of those in need. If there is no family to provide help, then the church is responsible. Notice this passage in *I Timothy 5:3-8 (NIV) ³ Give proper recognition to those widows who are really in need. ⁴ But if a widow has children or grandchildren, these should learn first of all to put their religion into practice by caring for their own family and so repaying their parents and grandparents, for this is pleasing to God. ⁵ The widow who is really in need and left all alone puts her hope in God and continues night and day to pray and to ask God for help. ⁶ But the widow who lives for pleasure is dead even while she lives. ⁷ Give the people these instructions, too, so that no one may be open to blame. ⁸ **If anyone does not provide for his relatives, and especially for his immediate family, he has denied the faith and is worse than an unbeliever.**

If we are unwilling to provide for our relatives who are unable to provide for themselves, the Bible says we have denied the faith. What is the fate of an unbeliever? Hell. If we do not provide for our family, our fate will be worse than an unbeliever.

Part of the reformation necessary in America is for families to begin providing for those who are "really in need," taking the responsibility away from the government. Yes, we will have to sacrifice some of the things that we want to be able to provide for others, but this is the call of the gospel. *1 John 3:16-17 (NIV) [16] This is how we know what love is: Jesus Christ laid down his life for us. And we ought to lay down our lives for our brothers. [17] If anyone has material possessions and sees his brother in need but has no pity on him, how can the love of God be in him?*

God expects parents to provide for their children, and in turn, children may need to provide for their parents. The family is also responsible for their relatives; cousins, aunts, uncles, nieces, nephews, etc… If within your family, you have someone who is unable to work and provide for their daily necessities, the family is to come together and support them.

3. We are to provide for those in need

Notice this passage in *1 Timothy 5:16 (NIV) [16] If any woman who is a believer has widows in her family, she should help them and not let the church be burdened with them, so that the church can help those widows who are really in need.*

From this passage we see two institutional responsibilities. The first refers to family government and how the woman is to provide for any widows in her family. The second is the responsibility of the church to provide for widows who do not have anyone to care for them. Notice there is no responsibility of the government to provide for those in need.

The church is made up of individuals and families. We are to provide for the needs of those who are unable to work. Families and churches are the appropriate welfare program.

Paul writes this to the church in Ephesus. *Ephesians 4:28 (NIV) [28] He who has been stealing must steal no longer, but must work, doing something useful with his own hands, that he may have something to share with those in need.* To steal is to take something that does not belong to you. If a person is able to work, and they receive assistance from another, they are stealing. Christians are not only to provide for their own necessities, but are also to have something to share with those in need.

The local church, when it comes together, is a powerful source for meeting the needs of a community. Let's say one family is able to give 50 dollars a month to help someone in need. What if ten families came together and gave the same amount? They would now have 500 dollars a month to give! The church is the storehouse for God's provisions. When we bring our tithes and offerings into the church, we need to be ministering to those in need in our communities. God's intention for the church has always been to help the poor.

Leviticus 25:35 (NIV) [35] "'If one of your countrymen becomes poor and is unable to support himself among you, help him as you would an alien or a temporary resident, so he can continue to live among you.

Deuteronomy 15:7-11 (NIV) [7] If there is a poor man among your brothers in any of the towns of the land that the LORD your God is giving you, do not be hardhearted or tightfisted toward your poor brother. [8] **Rather be openhanded and freely lend him whatever he needs.** *[9] Be careful not to harbor this wicked thought: "The seventh year, the year for canceling debts, is near," so that you do not show ill will toward your needy brother and give him nothing. He may then appeal to the LORD against you, and you will be found guilty of sin. [10] Give generously to him and do so without a grudging heart;* <u>**then because of this**</u> *the LORD your God will bless you in all your work and in everything you put your hand to. [11]* **There will always be poor people in the land. Therefore I command you to be openhanded toward your brothers and toward the poor and needy in your land.**

Many of us know of the terrible sins that Sodom and Gomorrah were committing just before God destroyed them. Ezekiel gives us insight as to why they were destroyed. *Ezekiel 16:49-50 (NIV) [49] "'Now this was the sin of your sister Sodom: She and her daughters were arrogant, overfed and unconcerned; <u>they did not help the poor and needy</u>. [50] They were haughty and did detestable things before me. Therefore I did away with them as you have seen.*

God will bless those who give generously without a grudging heart. This teaching about offering to help those in need is repeated in the New Testament. *2 Corinthians 9:6-8 (NIV) [6] Remember this: Whoever sows sparingly will also reap sparingly, and whoever sows generously will also reap generously. [7] Each man should give what he has decided in his heart to give, not reluctantly or under compulsion, for God loves a cheerful giver. [8] And God is able to make all grace abound to you, so that in all things at all times, having all that you need, you will abound in every good work.*

When Paul went to the Apostles to tell them of his call to take the gospel to the Gentiles, they commended him in his work and they told him to always remember the poor. *Galatians 2:10 (NIV) [10] All they asked was that we should continue to remember the poor, the very thing I was eager to do.*

Paul taught the church in Ephesus to work hard to provide for yourself and others. *Acts 20:34-35 (NIV) [34] You yourselves know that these hands of mine have* *supplied my own needs and the needs of my companions. ^{35} In everything I did, I showed you that by this kind of hard work we must help the weak, remembering the words the Lord Jesus himself said: 'It is more blessed to give than to receive.'"*

Jesus told us that the righteous who help people in need will be able to enter into heaven. The unrighteous who do not help people in need will go away to eternal punishment.

Matthew 25:34-46 (NIV) ^{34} "Then the King will say to those on his right, 'Come, you who are blessed by my Father; take your inheritance, the kingdom prepared for you since the creation of the world. ^{35} For I was hungry and you gave me something to eat, I was thirsty and you gave me something to drink, I was a stranger and you invited me in, ^{36} I needed clothes and you clothed me, I was sick and you looked after me, I was in prison and you came to visit me.' ^{37} "Then the righteous will answer him, 'Lord, when did we see you hungry and feed you, or thirsty and give you something to drink? ^{38} When did we see you a stranger and invite you in, or needing clothes and clothe you? ^{39} When did we see you sick or in prison and go to visit you?' ^{40} "The King will reply, 'I tell you the truth, whatever you did for one of the least of these brothers of mine, you did for me.' ^{41} "Then he will say to those on his left, 'Depart from me, you who are cursed, into the eternal fire prepared for the devil and his angels. ^{42} For I was hungry and you gave me nothing to eat, I was thirsty and you gave me nothing to drink, ^{43} I was a stranger and you did not invite me in, I needed clothes and you did not *clothe me, I was sick and in prison and you did not look after me.'* [44] *"They also will answer, 'Lord, when did we see you hungry or thirsty or a stranger or needing clothes or sick or in prison, and did not help you?'* [45] *"He will reply, 'I tell you the truth, whatever you did not do for one of the least of these, you did not do for me.'* [46] *"Then they will go away to eternal punishment, but the righteous to eternal life."*

We should not be overly judgmental or try to justify any decision not to help the poor or those in need. It is our responsibility is to help those who have made mistakes and can't help themselves. We do not want to be enablers and keep people dependent on others, but we must help them and teach them how to live productive lives.

Jesus did not say to just help the innocent prisoners. He commands us to remember those in prison and to cloth those in need. If we think things like, *"Well they deserved what they got,"* and choose to not help them, then we are deserving of Hell. The gospel tells us that we are all deserving of Hell. It is only because of God's mercy and grace that we are saved from what we really deserve. God shows unbelievable love and compassion that none of us deserve. We are to do the same for those who have messed up their lives and need help. Without God reaching out to us, we could not be saved! As we help others in need, we are displaying the gospel for all to see!

Within our earthly works we are to be great examples, hard workers, respectful, orderly, and diligent. We will look at these in more detail as we get into the responsibilities of family government.

Heavenly works

We not only have earthly works to accomplish, but we also have heavenly works that we are responsible to do. Paul told the church in Corinth in *I Corinthians 15:58 (NIV) [58] Therefore, my dear brothers, stand firm. Let nothing move you.* ***Always give yourselves fully to the work of the Lord****, because you know that your labor in the Lord is not in vain.*

In I Corinthians 9:1, Paul refers to the "work of the Lord" as in people getting saved and maturing because of his ministry.

Jesus said in, Matthew 9:36-38 (NIV) [36] When he saw the crowds, he had compassion on them, because they were harassed and helpless, like sheep without a shepherd. [37] Then he said to his disciples, "The harvest is plentiful but the workers are few. [38] Ask the Lord of the harvest, therefore, to send out workers into his harvest field."

The *"workers are few"* refers to those who will accept the call of the gospel to go and make disciples of all nations. God has commissioned us to work hard at teaching people to obey God's Word. The harvest is all the people who are harassed and helpless. These are people who are not saved and are not obeying all that Christ has commanded. Our nation is full of harassed and helpless people who need to hear the gospel and then follow God's Word in their lives.

Our nation is in a mess. Our country is out of order in obeying God's institutions of self, family, church, and civil government. Workers need to rise up and lay down their lives for the gospel. Not only are souls at stake, but the very freedoms we enjoy are at stake as well. Freedom is only found is Jesus and in obeying the responsibilities we have in His institutions. If we will repent and return to God and His Word, and teach others to do the same, we could see another Great Awakening. We need a reformation in our nation and all of God's workers to go out into the harvest field.

Our prayer is to see more workers who accept the call of God and begin teaching people to obey God's Word. You can use this Life Truth tool, another Biblical tool, or the Bible itself. It doesn't matter, the urgency is still the same. We must begin to study the Word ourselves and then teach it to others.

Look at what Paul tells Timothy in *2 Timothy 2:15 (NIV)* *15 Do your best to present yourself to God as one approved, a **workman** who does not need to be ashamed and who **correctly handles the word of truth.**

There are a lot of false teachings in our generation that need to be dealt with. We must learn to correctly handle the truth of God's Word.

God's will for all of us is to become like Christ. We are to study, memorize, meditate, and teach the Word of God. In looking over the Life Truths, we can see areas that we need to work on in self-government:

- Scripture alone is what governs me
- I need a new nature
- I must crucify my old nature
- I am created to serve
- I am created to praise
- I am created to encourage
- I am created to witness
- I am created to forgive
- I am created to be holy
- I am created to work

We are not only responsible to obey God's Word for ourselves but we are responsible for teaching God's Word to our families and to others. If you are not teaching someone else the Word of God, you are not fulfilling your heavenly works.

Many in the church today have become idle in their heavenly works. We must be diligent in going and in teaching the nations to obey. In the book of Amos, the nation of Israel had become lazy and comfortable.

They were idle in their obedience to God. The prophet Amos gave a stern warning to the nation about a judgment that would come for their disobedience.

Amos 6:4-7 (NIV) ⁴ You lie on beds inlaid with ivory and lounge on your couches. You dine on choice lambs and fattened calves. ⁵ You strum away on your harps like David and improvise on musical instruments. ⁶ You drink wine by the bowlful and use the finest lotions, **but you do not grieve over the ruin of Joseph.** *⁷ Therefore you will be among the first to go into exile; your feasting and lounging will end.*

In America, we have many luxuries and comforts. We like our entertainment and leisure time. This prophecy could be said about us in many ways. Their nation was not grieving over the ruin of Joseph. They were unconcerned about everyone else but themselves.

- Could the same be said of us?
- Are we concerned that America is falling apart?
- Are we willing to do something about it?

Just the fact that you have made it this far in reading this book tells me that you are committed to learning more about obeying Jesus and making a difference for Him. Don't make the mistake of thinking that the gospel is only for you and your family. The gospel is to be taken to the nations. Not just the message of praying a prayer asking Jesus into your heart, but the message of teaching them *"to obey all things"* like the commission states in Matthew 28:18-20. Bring another family into your home and begin learning the Self Government truths together. Then move on to the Family Government, Church Government, and Civil Government.

Will we sacrifice our wants to study the Word, memorize some verses, and then gather people together to teach them the Word of God?
Will we obey what Jesus commanded us to do?

If just a few families would commit to studying the Life Truths, and form Life Groups to teach the Truths to others, an awakening could occur in our communities.

What if 11 families began leading Life Groups? In just a few years, many families could be leading Life Groups and making disciples.

11 + 11 = 22 + 22 = 44 + 44 = 88 + 88 = 176

I'm excited about the possibilities of a revival in our community and a revival in our nation. I am praying for more workers.

If we spent time praying, studying the Word together, and then teaching the Word to just one family a year, we could see tremendous results.

We all make time for what we love. Look at what Jesus said in *John 14:15 (NIV)* *15 "If you love me, you will obey what I command.* If we love God, we need to become workers in the harvest field. We need to pray that more workers come who are willing to follow God's command to give themselves fully to the work of the Lord.

WORKSHEET FOR SELF-GOVERNMENT
LIFE TRUTH # 10
I AM CREATED TO WORK

Question: Does our old nature want to work?
Answer: No, it does not. We must crucify our old nature and learn to work.

> *1 Thessalonians 4:11-12 (NIV) 11 Make it your ambition to lead a quiet life, to mind your own business and to work with your hands, just as we told you, 12 so that your daily life may win the respect of outsiders and so that you will not be dependent on anybody.*
>
> Write out the Life Truth, question, and answer on one side of an index card and the verse on the other side. Keep it in your Bible for the week. Work on it every day individually and as a family. Have it memorized by next week.

Read 2 Thessalonians 3:6-12. Idle means: Not engaged in earning a living; depending on the labor and generosity of others for support. (Holman Bible Dictionary)

According to this passage God commands the church to keep away from whom?

We should warn people and teach them that they are to do what according to verse 12?

S_____ down and E_____ the B_____ they E_____.

Those who are able to work should work for three reasons:
To provide for themselves (2 Thessalonians 3:12)
To provide for their F_____ (1 Timothy 5:8)
To provide for the P_____ (Galatians 2:10)

Read Luke 14:12-14 According to this passage who should we give a luncheon for?

We are to work to provide for our daily necessities and we are to work in making disciples. What does the Holy Spirit call Paul's missionary journey in Acts 13:2,3? F_____ the W_____

Read Luke 10:1-20. How many did Jesus send out? He sent them T_____ by T_____
What is the harvest that Jesus is referring to?
According to verse 7, what work are they doing that deserves wages?
According to verse 17, what name did the demons submit to?
According to verse 19, how much power of the enemy can we overcome?
According to verse 20, why should we rejoice?

Based on this LIFE TRUTH what commitments do you need to make to be sure you are working? Work can be broken down into two parts: 1. Working to provide for daily necessities and to help others. 2. Working to advance the gospel. Which area do you need to work on most and why?